THE TRIAL OF THOMAS E. TOOLAN, III

MICHAEL WELLS GLUECK

Author:

Living Among The Swiss
The Retirement Home Experience
What I Learned At University
Neil Entwistle's Day In Court
The Nantucket Rape Trial
 Two 2019 Nantuckeyt Rape Trials
 Kevin Spacey's Aborted Trial

THE TRIAL OF THOMAS E. TOOLAN, III

ISBN-13:

All rights reserved

Copyright 2007, 2016, 2019, 2022

No part of this book may be reproduced or transmitted in any form or by any means, graphic, electronic, or mechanical, including photocopying, recording, taping, or by any information storage or retrieval system, without written permission from the author or publisher. +

Published by:
EditAndPublishYourBook.com
Michael Wells Glueck, Proprietor
E-mail: MichaelTheAuthor@GMail.com

In the early afternoon of Monday, October 25, 2004, the body of Elizabeth "Beth" Lochtefeld, age forty-four, was discovered lying prone on the floor of her rented cottage at 1A Hawthorne Lane on the island of Nantucket, Massachusetts. Some objects had been placed on her back; one of these was at first euphemistically described as "vegetative matter". Later that afternoon, Thomas E. Toolan III, age thirty-seven, who had worked in the financial industry in New York and elsewhere, was arrested in Rhode Island, his rented automobile cluttered with empty containers of vodka and beer. After waiving extradition, he was returned to Massachusetts and subsequently charged with premeditated first-degree murder committed with extreme and unusual cruelty, brutality, and atrocity. The beauty, vivacity, and successful entrepreneurship of the victim, who had managed her own real-estate consulting firm in New York, have been widely publicized, as has her sense that in Nantucket she would find the husband who never materialized during twenty years of living in New York. Her hortatory monograph, *Tell Me About Your Dreams* , containing illustrations by her father, was published posthumously. The focus of this account is upon the subsequent trial that began in Nantucket Superior Court on June 4, 2007. The presiding judge was the honorable Richard Connon; the prosecutor, assistant district attorney Brian Glenny, whose burden includes proving the defendant's volition or intention to commit the killing as well as his cognition or awareness of the criminal nature of the act; the defense attorney, Kevin Reddington of Brocton, Massachusetts, who according to Hilary Russ, a reporter for *The Cape Cod Times, is regarded by* experts as one of the top five defense lawyers in the Commonwealth — even though he has reportedly not won every case he undertook. Mr. Reddington elected to pursue a defense of diminished capacity by reason of insanity caused by alcoholism and drug abuse and aggravated by the defendant's rejection by the victim. Reddington noted, and one of the victim's brothers has confirmed that Toolan had proposed marriage and that the couple had spoken of starting a family. Of course, short of adoption, it would not have been such an easy matter for a hitherto childless woman of Ms. Lochtefeld's age to conceive, say, a Thomas E. Toolan IV, but there are reports that she was taking folic acid supplements in an effort to increase her fertility. If the defendant were found guilty of all of the charges, he would likely be sentenced to life imprisonment without the possibility of parole — the outcome sought by the prosecution. If the jury were to accept the insanity theory, however, the defendant might be found guilty of second-degree murder or of voluntary manslaughter, be sentenced to a less severe prison term, and eventually become eligible for parole; or, if he were acquitted outright, he would probably be committed to a mental institution, as was John Hinckley, Jr., the assailant of former President Ronald Reagan. The first four days of the trial were devoted to jury selection. In the late afternoon of the third day, the judge denied defense counsel's motion for a change of venue, and the attorney immediately appealed to the state's highest court. On Thursday morning a single justice of that court denied the appeal without referring it to the full court. He also denied a hitherto secret motion to sequester the jury. One suspects that economics and a disinclination to establish a precedent against murder trials being held on Nantucket motivated these decisions. That same afternoon, in less than an hour a jury of thirteen women and three men, including four alternates, was selected before the pool of potential jurors had been exhausted. Apparently, defense counsel, who had complained to the judge that the proceeding was "flirting with being a hollow formality," perceived no alternative but to play his role in the putative farce. Like the victim and the defendant, all the jurors are Caucasian. Casually attired in the usual Nantucket manner, they are the local embodiment of a jury of the expensively dressed defendant's peers. One wonders whether after the conclusion of the trial the defendant will ever again have occasion to wear such finery. He is arguably lucky that the Commonwealth of Massachusetts has no death penalty. Opening statements began on the morning of the fifth day of the trial. The defense attorney noted that the defendant was wearing a nice suit and didn't look crazy, but that prior to incarceration he had drunk a daily fifth of Absolut vodka straight from the bottle without apparent difficulty. He appealed to jurors' common sense and sympathy, provoking an objection from the prosecutor and a bench conference that resulted in the judge advising jurors: "You may feel natural emotions, but you may not let them influence your verdict, which must be based solely on he evidence presented — exhibits and witness testimony." The judge also instructed the jury not to draw inferences from a failure of the defendant to testify on his own behalf, not to discuss the case among themselves or with others, and not to look at related media reports. Standing while jurors filed in and out of the courtroom, I recognized none of them even after living on the island for a decade. For the past thirty-one months of imprisonment, the defendant has presumably imbibed not even a single alcoholic beverage. This may be good for his liver, but prison food may have offsetting effects, such as Michael Milken's inoperable prostate cancer or Jack Kevorkian's cirrhosis. Exhibits included gory photographs of the deceased victim lying prone and bleeding profusely, with blood on her hands and clothing; the garments were also shown. The defense attorney asked only a few questions of three of the witnesses, and he stipulated as to the photographs. The witnesses included the victim's brother, who had expected her to pick up his son at a nearby school on the day she was killed, and who had called 911 after his sister's landlady had finally reached him after an hour of trying to do so; two police officers who were the first authorities to arrive at the murder scene and who, after one of them looked through a window and saw a motionless body lying on the floor, gained entrance by kicking in a door; neighbors, all of whom commented on the defendant's rented car being parked on the wrong side of a road on which no parked cars were normally seen; the medical examiner, who found no vital signs on the body and signed the death certificate; the victim's landlady, who had invited her tenant to help her dig up some sweet potatoes on what proved to be the afternoon of the murder. The landlady knew the victim's parents – who were present in the courtroom every day and who own a local art gallery that also functions as a sales outlet for on-island concerts – before she rented her cottage to the victim in March of 2003. (The cottage is currently rented and occupied.) The victim's brother had helped his sister carry in some of her Manhattan furniture. The defendant's parents, retired schoolteachers who founded and ran a Montessori school in New York, were in daily attendance, elegantly attired and sitting in a different section from the one occupied by the victim's family; there was understandably no interaction between the two groups. Presumably, the elder Toolans were helping to pay for both the attorney and his jury consultant from Beverly Hills, California. The ordeal seemed to be especially hard on the father, whose frequent trips to the restroom pointed to a possible prostate problem. His wife was especially solicitous toward him. Toward her son, she appeared to be indignantly reproachful. According to the *New York Post reporter, the defendant could not* meet her scornful gaze. It is said that a man's attitude toward his mother influences his treatment of women generally. The jury was taken to view the cottage where the slaying occurred, along with one store where the defendant sought and another where he purchased two knives, the airport median where the victim's wallet was found. I joined members of the press on the sandy lane outside the cottage, but no one except the judge and the jurors were permitted to enter it or the grounds. Back in the courtroom after the viewing, witnesses commented on the defendant's long gray topcoat and fedora hat and sunglasses. The victim's cell phone was found in the defendant's overcoat pocket, along with a hitherto undisclosed second knife, a small scallop utensil – not the murder weapon, which has not been located. His own scarf was also found in a pocket of the coat. The presence of the cell phone recalls his previous arrest for attempting to steal an eighty-thousand dollar bust of Julius Caesar from a Manhattan antiques show. The victim's blood was found on the defendant's clothing and in his car and was DNA-tested to confirm it was hers. In a frenzy of gross overkill that began in a bedroom and ended in the living room as she tried in vain to fight off and to escape her attacker, she had been stabbed twenty-three times. (This number would be repeated like a mantra throughout the trial.) There was no mention of the defendant's DNA, of which two samples had been taken since his arrest on the day of the murder, October 25, 200 Only the victim's brother positively identified the defendant; the landlady and other neighbors had given him only cursory glances on the day of the crime, and thus they were not even asked whether he was the person whom they saw on the day of the killing. Present were representatives of the Associated Press, the *New York Post*, *People Magazine*, *ABC's internet services* division, CBS' *48 Hours*, NBC's *Dateline*, Court TV, *The Cape Cod Times*, *The Nantucket Inquirer and Mirror*, *The Nantucket Independent*, *and National* Public Radio, all of whom I met, including both journalists and photographers. A *New York Post reporter sitting in the next* seat mini-interviewed me, asking why I was there and subsequently what my published books' titles are. The defendant seldom looked at the proceedings to his near left and never at the jurors to his far left, but usually looked away to his right, even when his attorney was not seated next to him on that side. This was especially true during presentations of graphic or gory photographs. The pained expression on his face was a mixture of obstinate aversion, disgust, and contempt — but not a trace of regret or remorse. The defendant lied to Rhode Island police who pulled him over: after prodding them to explain the cause of his arrest and eliciting that it had to do with the victim, he claimed that he hadn't seen her for the past three days. The defense attorney emphasized that the defendant was not what he seemed, comparing him with Michael Douglas in the movie "Falling Down" and with Russell Crowe in the film "A Beautiful Mind." He commented, "You don't have to have somebody with a beanie on his head and a little whirligig going around to be insane." Notwithstanding its faulty syntax, this epigram proved to be the quotation of the day. the sixth day of the trial produced startling revelations. In response to prodding by the defense attorney in what may have been an attempt to impugn the victim's morality, a state pathologist disclosed that the "vegetative matter" found on Ms. Lochtefeld's back was, to a reasonable scientific certainty even though not tested, marijuana. The other objects, revealed to the general public but presumably not to the jurors in a sensational *New York Post story by* reporter Jack Coleman, were identified as a vibrating dildo, a battery pack to operate it, and K-Y lubricant jelly. Mr. Coleman being the reporter from that newspaper whom I had met the preceding Friday, I asked him about those items and gleaned the additional detail, not published in the edited article, that the dildo was pink. As the article does indicate, these items were presumably placed on the victim's back by the defendant for the police to find, and their intended purpose was obviously to denigrate the slain woman. The witness also conceded that the bruises on Ms. Lochtefeld's legs might well have been caused by falling and striking a a. piece of furniture or other object. In response to questions from the prosecutor, the pathologist revealed that while there had been no sexual penetration of the victim's vagina or anus, her publc hair had been shaved. I asked a free-lance reporter for *People Magazine about the purpose of the* question, and was told that Brian McDonald's 2006 book *Safe Harbor: A Murder In Nantucket characterizes the* defendant as a kinky type who women from previous attachments complained had assaulted them with sex toys of this type, by shaving their pubic hair, and by inundating them with what the pulp fiction writers generally term "golden showers." Since it is known that Ms. Lochtefeld went to New York to tell Mr. Toolan personally that she was ending their relationship, and that he kept her in his apartment for a time against her will, there is speculation that he practiced at least some of these perversions, including the nether shaving, upon her as well. After she managed to escape in the early morning hours and to return to Nantucket, she asked police about the procedure for obtaining a restraining order but didn't follow up. On Sunday night, I had anonymously e-mailed the defense attorney areminder that the prosecution had not mentioned the defendant's DNA, of which two samples had been taken with his consent during his long incarceration. Perhaps coincidentally, perhaps not, on Monday afternoon the attorney also asked the pathologist whether various surfaces on items found at the victim's cottage, the airport, or the two cars rented from Budget by the defendant that had been swabbed for fingerprints or handprints had also been tested for DNA. The answers were generally negative. The Ford Escape left in the appropriate parking area of the Nantucket airport without being checked in or its keys returned (found among Mr. Toolan's possessions in Rhode Island) contained a plastic bag that held three unopened bottles of Beck's beer as well as one empty bottle of the same brand. In a trash container at the airport police found a luggage tag with Mr. Toolan's name on it, as well as a plastic bag with some art slides from Ms. Lochtefeld's collection. The victim's wallet was spotted lying in some bushes on a median strip in front of the main entrance to the airport. The members of the jury (but not the spectators) were subjected to detailed descriptions of each of the twenty-three wounds inflicted upon the victim in regard to length, edge sharpness, depth, and directional orientation, as well as to graphic, close-up photographs of the wounds on all portions of the victim's unclothed body. Any one of six of those wounds, several experts testified, could have proved fatal. There were more wounds in the right lung than in the left, and the autopsy showed that Ms. Lochtefeld's heart was neither injured by the assault nor diseased. Her death was caused by a combination of massive blood loss and trauma to her damaged lungs, and clearly fell into the category of homicide. One cannot help wondering whether she could have been saved had the landlady called 911 immediately instead of attempting for an hour to reach the victim's elder brother. Undoubtedly the landlady, who has been attending the trial sessions, has asked herself that question innumerable times. At the defense attorney's request, the judge advised jurors that although it was necessary to show the gory photographs they should not allow related revulsion or other emotions or sympathy for either side to influence their verdict, which had to be based solely upon the evidence. In response to the defense attorney's question about 'frenzy killings," the pathologist described the areas and functions of the brain, and agreed with Mr. Reddington that damage to the frontal lobes, which control thought and emotions including impulse control, can be detected by CT or MRI scans or by neurosis testing. The implications of this line of questioning for the insanity plea were obvious. It was disclosed that the defendant had spent time at two rehabilitation facilities, one called Silver Hill Hospital in New Canaan, Connecticut, and the second, where he stayed on two occasions, named Hazelton for the town of that name in Minnesota. Another patient surnamed Keegan whose stay at Hazelton had briefly coincided with Mr. Toolan's testified about their mutual supportiveness and encouragement whenever one of them "fell off the wagon." He said that the defendant had asked him to call Ms. Lochtefeld at seven o'clock on the evening of the killing, but without his cell phone was unable to provide the number; then called him back an hour later to ask if he had been able to reach her, and, upon being answered in the negative, told him "not to worry about it." The witness, noted that his friend had sounded much more inebriated, depressed, and inarticulate than at six o'clock on the previous evening — the day before the slaying — when Mr. Toolan had telephoned him from a bar and, though seemingly upbeat, had admitted that his relationship with the victim was not going well. Mr. Keegan advised his friend to take a taxi home. He never spoke again with the defendant, who, he said, sometimes disappeared for months and then resurfaced. This testimony, too, was elicited by Mr. Reddington in apparent support of his insanity theory, and he frequently referred to his client as "Tom" in what seemed a patent effort to humanize him. Both the owner of a shipping company and his female clerk identified the package containing Mr. Toolan's personal belongings that Ms. Lochtefeld had left there to be shipped back via United Parcel Service but that had been intercepted by the Nantucket police. The clerk described the forty-four year-old Ms. Lochtefeld as "a young lady." Throughout the testimony on this day, the defendant took no notes, occasionally riffled through legal papers or conferred with his lawyer, but otherwise sat forlorn and motionless, usually directing his glance away from the jury, witness stand, and exhibits while the drama played out around him. The prosecutor was methodical, patient, determined, and thorough, cumulatively eliciting a steamroller of detailed testimony of the presumptive and actual presence of blood, with only occasional polite interruptions and objections by the defense attorney, who, however, did demonstrate through cross-examination that not all of the untested blood found in the kitchen was necessarily human, and that blood found in the bathroom could have been naturally discharged from various orifices. After the day's session had concluded, I wended my way to a local bookshop and purchased a copy of Brian McDonald's book about the case. More forensic testimony dominated the seventh day of the trial. Letters placed on the bed after the killing that had become stained with blood were introduced, as were all the items recovered at La Guardia Airport, including the blue towel-wrapped kitchen knife concealed in a pocket of a trench coat, which was also produced. After the knife was discovered, Mr. Toolan alternately said that he'd forgotten it was in his coat pocket, then that his sister in Nantucket had asked him to bring it to help cut a turkey dinner, then a fish dinner, then a birthday cake, and then to clean any fish he caught while on the island. He also offered inappropriately to reward the screener for his vigilance. Another screener noticed that the subject's fly was unzipped. More than three years after September 11, 2001, it is incomprehensible that the defendant thought he could get the knife through security. A female friend of the victim from San Diego, California drove up to Marina del Rey in Los Angeles after Labor Day of 2004 to meet Ms. Lochtefeld when Mr. Toolan brought her along on a business trip and testified that her friend was happy at the time but not long afterward complained that "the relationship had changed dramatically for the worse." Actually, this last phrase was agreed to by opposing counsel with the judge's approval after the witness' clear reluctance to answer any questions from the defense caused her to stammer unresponsively. Items found in the two cars rented by the victim from Budget in Nantucket and Hyannis included keys to his Lexus, a suit coat bearing the label of an upscale New York men's store, Paul Stuart, other items of clothing including some with bloodstains, two pairs of brown shoes, bottles of human anti-depressant tablets and canine anti-anxiety pills ("for thunderstorms," which frightened the defendant's white German shepherd), empty and mostly full bottles of Absolut vodka, empty and full bottles of Beck's beer, a pack of Winston cigarettes. Winston butts had also been found on the floor in a bedroom of Ms. Lochtefeld's rented cottage. As the defense attorney, alluding to Tom Wolfe's *The Bonfire Of The Vanities* , had previously characterized him, the defendant had been "a master of the universe," handsomely paid by Salomon Smith Barney, where he was a vice president, and also by Citicorp, where he worked for a week before getting into a drunken altercation at a party hosting investment bankers from Merrill Lynch, Morgan Stanley and other firms and being fired the following morning, a Friday. The prosecutor was once again dogged and methodical in producing items of evidence that cumulatively added up to a small mountain. At one point, the scallop knife was placed on an evidence table within the defendant's reach, but he made no move to seize it and acted as if he were unaware of its position, even though the courtroom guards were unarmed. After lunch, there was a break in the testimony while a twenty-one minute video was shown without the accompanying audio, which the police official who had operated the camera described malapropistically as "extemporaneous noise." (He meant extraneous noise.) Other Spoonerisms included the defense counsel's repeated use of "lay" for "lie" and the judge's daily confirmation that the jury remained "indifferent," legal jargon for impartial and unbiased.) The video depicted the victim's lifeless, bloodstained body lying on the floor of the living room after the objects that had been placed on her back had been removed, as well as bloodstains in other rooms and in both rental cars. Tellingly, several of the jurors averted their glances from the monitor, unable to look at the gory scenes. Especially in the absence of any expression of remorse or regret, this does not augur well for the defendant, who continued to direct his forlorn glances away from the courtroom drama. He even betrayed no reaction when some of his letters and e-mails to Ms. Lochtefeld were read aloud by his counsel. Examples: "And then it is the screaming, real or no, seems so" when the relationship was rocky; "Placid is the dull rose with the red sung through," when their love seemed to blossom. After the killing, the defendant is said to have lain on the victim's bed and reread some of these verses. On the eighth day of the trial, the defendant and the jurors avoided looking at each other. Referring to the canine pills seized from the defendant's travel bag in Rhode Island, the defense attorney noted that sometimes people take them "to get high" and questioned whether the existence of the veterinarian who wrote the prescription had been verified. Also seized were the defendant's olive green trenchcoat and gray overcoat, a dress shirt, a tie, and shoes; an amethyst ring; vitamins; various prescription medicines, most but not all Class E controlled substances, such as Zoloft antidepressant tablets and a tranquilizer that also acts as a venal block for pulse reduction; and a single condom. A press representative behind me commented, "He had a rolling drugstore." A Nantucket airport employee reported that Mr. Toolan had accidentally walked into the ladies' room, perceived his mistake, turned and left. Prosecutor: "And what did you do next?" Giggling: "I went to the bathroom." When he'd arrived at Nantucket Airport and proceeded to the Budget rental counter, the agent said she'd had a reservation for him the previous evening, and the defendant — continuing his pattern of ready lies — said that he'd been delayed in traffic, missed his flight, and slept overnight at LaGuardia Airport. Mr. Toolan had also told a Rhode Island investigator that he'd injured his left calf, but there was no visible injury. Also in Rhode Island on the evening of the murder, he said that he hadn't eaten for forty-eight hours, when he'd had a slice of pizza, and that he hadn't slept since Saturday night, when he'd logged six hours. The investigator noted that his interlocutor's heart was racing, and that his blood alcohol level – first taken two hours after the arrest – was more than twice the legal limit. After acknowledging that he'd drunk four and one-half beers and had taken two swigs from an Absolut vodka bottle, and after failing most of the physical sobriety tests as well, the defendant was issued a citation for driving under the influence of alcohol. He refused to sign a prisoner intake form but did sign in a wavering script a notification of legal rights form. He wore soft contact lenses. All the Rhode Island authorities testified that the defendant, notwithstanding his proven intoxication, responded appropriately (and walked normally without assistance) except when he was ordered at gunpoint to unlock the rental car at the roadblock near Warwick and to show his hands. For a time, they said, he merely stared at them; four repeated commands were required before he complied. When eventually told that the matter concerned Ms. Lochtefeld, Mr. Toolan said that the matter had nothing to do with him because he hadn't seen "Beth" since Friday. He learned no more about the charges at that time because he refused to waive his right not to answer questions, although, as noted, he did receive and acknowledge his Miranda rights. None of this points to an insane person. The defense counsel asked the top Rhode Island crime services investigator, whose credentials he first carefully established, what had become of a pillbox upon which some bloodstains had been traced. The investigator said he had given the pillbox to the Massachusetts state police and didn't know what they had done with it but thought it was still in their custody. Told that it had been returned to Mr. Toolan, he shrugged and said it wasn't his responsibility. Counsel: "And you are the senior crime services investigator for the state of Rhode Island, correct?" "That's correct." "No further questions." It was disclosed that it took Mr. Toolan six years to earn his bachelor's degree. A friend and squash/tennis partner of the defendant's, the well-spoken Mark Mitchell, testified that Mr. Toolan had gone "on the wagon" in December 2003 upon the advice of a physician, who noted that his triglycerides were elevated and his liver inflamed. At Mr. Toolan's invitation, he continued, they had spent Labor Day weekend on Nantucket, staying with a female friend of the defendant who — doubtless to her everlasting regret — introduced him to Ms. Lochtefeld after telephoning her with a quickly acted- upon invitation to come over because "I may be looking at your future husband." The defendant told Mr. Mitchell that he'd begun to ease back into drinking beer again with his doctor's approval and was ready to try some vodka, which, however, burned his stomach to the point that he desisted. The weather was sunny and warm, the company happy, the couple clearly in love. Beth Lochtefeld seemed finally to have found Mr. Goodbar. But euphoria is evanescent. Around noon on a Saturday seven weeks later, Mr. Mitchell received a call from Mr. Toolan asking him to join him at the New York Athletics Club, of which both were members. He did so, found the usually dapper and sartorially proper Mr. Toolan at the bar, sloppily dressed to the point of dishevelment with stained trousers, intoxicated, severely depressed and speaking in an uncommonly loud voice about the breakup with Ms. Lochtefeld. Then he briefly lost track of his friend, but found him on the roof standing near the edge and contemplating a jump. Uttering "bromides," he pulled the defendant away from the roof's edge and brought him back downstairs. He then took Mr. Toolan home, where he saw him drinking vodka straight out of a bottle in his bathroom. Mr. Mitchell took it away from him, then gave up and returned it. His friend took another swig or two, then poured some down the sink, turned toward the living room, and relaxed on the couch. In that room a long conversation ensued. The defendant told him that Ms. Lochtefeld had broken up with him because of his drinking and removed her possessions from his apartment. He'd told her that he represented her last chance to have a baby. She had been staying in New York at a former boyfriend's apartment. They talked about drinking and drugs, and Mr. Toolan said he hadn't had any cocaine in at least fifteen years. Sensing his friend's depression, Mr. Mitchell took him to an hour-long Alcoholics Anonymous meeting that same night, October 23, making the arrangement through a sponsor of Mr. Toolan, who had clearly attended AA meetings before. They then walked toward Mr. Toolan's West End Avenue apartment (around Eightieth Street), encountered three young women along the way, but resisted the usual temptation to invite them out for a drink. Continuing their stroll, Mr. Mitchell at least twice dissuaded his friend from entering a bar for a beer, but Mr. Toolan then said he needed a drink, entered a liquor store, and purchased a pint of Ketel One vodka, which Mr. Mitchell wrested away from him when the dog was distracted. The defendant then bought another pint of vodka, and the now-alert dog (who "did not take kindly to my incursions upon his master") prevented Mr. Mitchell from seizing it as well. But after arriving at the apartment, he pushed the dog out of the elevator, closed the door, seized the vodka, stashed it in a corner of the lobby, and joined his friend upstairs, where they chatted. Around midnight, Mr. Toolan called his mother. About fifteen minutes after two o'clock on Saturday morning, Mr. Toolan passed out on his bed, and Mr. Mitchell then left. On Sunday, he tried to contact the defendant by telephone and e-mail, but received no response. He never saw him again until today in the courtroom, when Mr. Toolan did not look at him. While waiting to testify, Mr. Mitchell had told me that the defendant has been kept in solitary confinement for the past eighteen months — perhaps for his own protection as the growing mound of evidence against him became known to other inmates — but that he has responded to a few letters. On the stand, Mr. Mitchell said he thought his friend was a psychiatric case, and that he hadn't visited him at the prison. A full three days after the murder, he said, he had been contacted by state police. He said he'd never seen the defendant wearing a hat, which therefore may have either a means of shielding his eyes from the sun or else a disguise. He said that they seldom spoken about work, but that Mr. Toolan had mentioned been employed by Union Bank of Switzerland, Mellon Bank and other firms, and sometimes had boasted about lucrative deals in progress. The defendant continued not to look at his friend during this testimony. Throughout the day, he looked only at the attractive woman from the Watersports store Force 5, where he'd first tried to buy a knife, at the elderly part-time employee at Brant Point Marine, where he'd actually purchased the two knives, and at exhibits held up virtually in front of him. The Force 5 saleswoman said she'd found him frightening because of his formal clothing, the fact that he kept his hands in his pockets most of the time, and his failure to make eye contact with her when she'd greeted him as he entered the shop. The Brant Point Marine salesman (who looked overfed and overwatered) said he'd considered the defendant overdressed, and that, in another lie, Mr. Toolan told him that the airline had lost his luggage and that he accordingly needed to replace a lost scallop knife. Both sales clerks identified the defendant as the man who had come into the shops by pointing to him. A member of the Barnstable district attorney's office who sat next to me when not helping to operate the video player confirmed that male inmates at the Barnstable House Of Corrections see no female inmates (housed in a separate facility) or guards. This helps to explain Mr. Toolan's visible (and visceral) response to attractive female witnesses. If Massachusetts state prisons are similarly segregated, once the trial is over, he may see no women, other than any who visit him, for a long time to come. On the eighth day of the trial, the judge ran an especially strict courtroom. Observers were reprimanded for cupping their ears to hear soft-spoken witnesses who ignored the judge's instructions to "speak up," for opening or closing windows without authorization, or for closing their eyes, and were glared at for coughing or sneezing. One especially loud cough interrupted the testimony. His Honor even micromanaged the numbering of exhibits, which to date total more than one hundred. Security was tight, although no one's shoes matched the profile requiring removal before passing through the metal detector. Even the prosecutor had to ask permission to place the videocassettes into evidence before rewinding them. Before Day Nine of the trial began, I happened to bump into Mr. Reddington at the entrance to the town building. I described the e-mail I had sent him, and he acknowledged receiving it. Day Nine atypically seemed to include an unusual number of sidebar conferences. A video with partial audio was shown of the events in Rhode Island. The jury heard Mr. Toolan's voice for what will probably be the only time in this trial, but what they heard seemed unlikely to help his cause. While riding in the police cruiser with his hands cuffed behind him, his seat belt repeatedly came undone, and at one point the trooper pulled over, stopped the car, and patted him down again. In a deep baritone voice, the jurors heard him say the following: "I didn't do anything. I didn't do a goddamned thing. I didn't do a fucking thing [repeated once]. I'm just sitting here, I swear to God. On my honor, I didn't do anything." The obscenities may reflect the defendant's career in the financial industry, where traders and others think nothing of uttering the f-word in front of female colleagues. I think that defense counsel should find a way of explaining this to the jurors. Throughout the ninth day, the defendant sat hunched over or swaying, rarely looking at the proceedings — except during the testimonies of an attractive policewoman with whom he had spoken at the airport in Hyannis and of an equally fetching female DNA analyst from the Massachusetts state police crime laboratory. Her presentation was so compelling that the judge stepped down from the bench to gain a better view. It seemed fitting that a determined female analyst (with a degree in molecular biology earned at the University of Connecticut's main campus in Storrs) provided the DNA-matching evidence that seems likely to help convict Mr. Toolan. The odds against the bloodstains found in the apartment (and on paper towels found in a trash container at the airport) belonging to anyone other than the victim or the defendant, she testified were quadrillions (millions of billions) to one. (A quadrillion is a one followed by fifteen zeroes.) Fingernail scrapings taken from both of the victim's hands confirmed the DNA match with exactly the same exponential odds she averred, pointing out that there are only about six billion people in the world. Attending the trial at various times were the chief Nantucket police detective; a former prosecutor, police chief, and retired attorney after whom a town building that he financed is named; senior members of the local bar;

and vacationing tourists who, like me, had never previously been present at a murder trial. These included a retired couple from Falmouth, a Pennsylvania court reporter and his wife, and a young couple with two children. The prosecutor, exhibiting unbounded energy, gave them a good show except during the long periods of videos without sound. At one point a sergeant with the Massachusetts state police subtly corrected the defense attorney by substituting "lying" for "laying." The defendant's parents were present at all times and were sometimes accompanied by a woman who appeared to be his sister. Likewise, the victim's brothers and usually her parents and friends were in attendance. None of Mr. Toolan's friends, including witnesses Keegan and Mitchell, observed the trial proceedings, doubtless not wishing to appear sympathetic to him under the circumstances. When Massachusetts state police officials interviewed Mr. Toolan in Rhode Island several hours after his breathalyzer tests, he still appeared to them to be intoxicated, his eyes glassy, and his breath reeking of alcoholic beverages. Massachusetts police, accompanied by New York officers, also searched the defendant's Manhattan apartment, noting its messiness and the abundance of empty Absolut vodka bottles. They were admitted by Mr. Toolan's female dog walker, who kept a key to the dwelling. The two DNA tests of Mr. Toolan were finally described, but only as to methodology, not as to utilization. Prescriptions for tranquilizers and anti-depressants signed by physicians named Everett Eccles, Richard Neufeld, and Robert Romanoff were introduced. This time Mr. Reddington did not question whether the signers actually existed. The number of exhibits admitted into evidence now exceeds one hundred thirty. Photographs and various documents were "published" — i.e., shown — to the jurors, who passed them along to one another while testimony continued. The judge twice instructed the jurors that they must consider the degree and quality of volition in the case of statements made by the defendant while intoxicated. The courtroom guards appeared to be unarmed but brooked no delays. Whenever they were ready to escort the defendant from the courtroom, he was obliged to leave almost immediately, even if conferring with his attorney. Reflecting upon the progress of the trial to date, it occurred to me that defense counsel should attempt the arduous task of painting a picture for the jury of how an eventually rehabilitated Mr. Toolan could resume a constructive role in society. What safeguards would there be against a relapse into alcoholism and violence? Who would hire him? Certainly not Wall Street firms. If he formed a company of his own, who would do business with him? It may be a stretch, but perhaps, in the manner of reformed imposter Frank W. Abagnale, Jr. author of *Catch Me If You Can and* other works, Mr. Toolan could become a crusader against alcoholism and travel around the country giving paid speeches. I e-mailed these thoughts along with the suggestion about the pervasiveness of foul language in Wall Street firms to Mr. Reddington, who kindly acknowledged receiving them and promised to consider them. The tenth day of the trial was occupied by the testimony of Dr. Martin J. Kelly, a senior and very well accredited forensic psychiatrist who has testified at more than one hundred murder trials, usually but not always for the district attorney's office. He has been cross- examined several times in the past by Attorney Kevin Reddington, who once obtained a ruling from the Commonwealth's Supreme Judicial court authorizing the videotaping of an interview with a defendant in such a trial. Subsequently, defense attorneys have been able to apply for similar authorizations in other such trials, and the procedure has become known as a "Kelly motion." Mr. Reddington: "Did you know that such motions are called 'Kelly motions'?" Dr. Kelly: "I've never heard it calledthat, but I'm honored." Testifying for the prosecution, Dr. Kelly not surprisingly opined that the defendant knew that his deadly assault upon the victim was wrong and illegal, that he did not have a mental disease or defect at the time of the attack, and that he possessed the capability of choosing to conform or not to conform his conduct to the requirements of the law. With the kind permission of *The Cape Cod Times* , I quote extensively from Hilary Russ' account in the online edition of *The Cape Cod Times Saturday, June 16, 2007:* "Prosecutors wrapped up their case yesterday with a doctor who claimed that although Thomas Toolan III had a substance abuse problem, he knew what he was doing — and that it was wrong — when he allegedly stabbed ex-girlfriend Elizabeth "Beth" Lochtefeld to death in October 200 "Forensic psychiatrist Martin Kelly told jurors Toolan did not have a "mental disease or defect" on the day of the killing. Toolan's defense attorney, Kevin Reddington, will try to argue his client was not "criminally responsible" for the slaying because a combination of factors — long-term substance abuse, anti- depressants and alcohol, a mental defect, and stress from his breakup with Lochtefeld — caused him either not to understand the wrongfulness of his alleged acts or to lack the ability to control his behavior. "Kelly said Toolan deliberately stabbed Lochtefeld twenty-three times, placed marijuana and other "items" on her back, disposed of the knife he had allegedly used, scattered Lochtefeld's purse and other items, and took a plane and rented a car to get away. "Toolan did appear to have "a mixed personality disorder with narcissistic and anti-social features," Kelly said, but that didn't prevent the thirty-nine year-old from making conscious choices about his behavior. "What's more, Kelly said some of Toolan's alleged actions — including giving LaGuardia Airport security different excuses why he tried to sneak a knife through security the night before the killing — showed that 'he's conforming his conduct to his self- interest at that moment' to cover up his alleged crime. "In an intense cross-examination, Reddington tried to eviscerate Kelly's credibility by cataloguing some of the one hundred fifty or so other grisly cases in which he has testified over the past three decades, including several in which he went up against Reddington before. Over and over, Reddington, reading from a list, rattled off cases in which Kelly had been a witness, mostly for prosecutors. "To reach his findings, Kelly conducted a nearly three-hour interview with Toolan at the Barnstable County Correctional Facility. "He also reviewed medical and police reports and hospital records of three admissions to two different drug and alcohol treatment centers in 1999 and 2001. "Toolan has been on Celexa and Zoloft, which are in a class of drugs the Food and Drug Administration flagged for risk of suicide in 2004, Kelly said. Also yesterday, "Toolan's primary care physician from 1999 to 2004 in Manhattan, Richard Neufeld, said the dosage of Toolan's Zoloft, which had been prescribed for performance anxiety during Toolan's business presentations, had been doubled four months before he allegedly killed Lochtefeld. "Toolan has also taken Buspar and Clonazepam, Kelly said. Toolan started drinking at age twelve and smoking marijuana at age thirteen, Kelly testified under cross-examination. He had frequent reported blackouts, stole three cars, and attempted suicide as a teenager with Valium and vodka after a girlfriend broke up with him, Kelly said. And he exhibited obsessive- compulsive behavior, including washing his hands, which had become red and raw, up to forty times a day [— a perversion of the axiom that cleanliness is next to godliness —] and frequently checking the exact placement of items in his apartment. "When prosecutor Brian Glenny asked follow-up queries, Kelly said a medical record showed that Toolan 'has a strong urge to want to control situations, especially relationships.'" The doctor acknowledged that

Mr. Toolan was understandably suspicious of his motives and indicated that group therapy is the best treatment for compulsive behavior disorders, even if the group consists of hypochondriacs who initially compete to be the sickest. In general, obsessive-compulsive behavior is clearly a question of degree. Many normal people who do not commit killings or other crimes wash their hands frequently, whether from guilt about masturbation during puberty or from a preoccupation with cleanliness. Indeed, many physicians advise washing one's hands before touching one's eyes, to reduce the possibility of contracting a common cold or influenza, and before eating, to avoid ingestion of harmful bacteria and viruses. Similarly, the defendant's desire to please people and his fear or suspicion that they were "out to get him" is present to some degree in many people who manage to function normally throughout their lives. And where exactly is the line between covering one's back and paranoia? Mr. Reddington — whose faux pas included use of "axises" and "diagnosises" instead of "axes" and "diagnoses" as the plurals of "axis" and "diagnosis," "stupefication" instead of "stupefaction," and who seemed to be under the false impression that Drugstore.com was at that time an unauthorized source of prescription medications, until he was disabused of that notion by Dr. Kelly, yet who, however, incorrectly stated that that online company sold only over-the-counter sundries such as toothpaste and not prescription drugs — accused this witness of not performing insufficient research upon the defendant's medical history (such as his recent weight loss, which can signify a mental illness) and brushes with the law, although Dr. Kelly knew that the parents had denied abusing their son and had read the reports from Hazelton: "You didn't care, did you? You were interested only in collecting your check, correct?" "No, that's not correct." This sarcasm may have backfired with the jurors; a female resident of Nantucket and former librarian sitting next to me murmured, "I think he's lost the jury." In contrast, the prosecutor successfully rehabilitated the witness by eliciting the information that on three occasions when the psychiatrist had been retained by the district attorney's office he had found the defendant not responsible for his or her actions. Mr. Glenny's presentation was candid and transparent, his treatment of witnesses invariably respectful, and these attributes seemed to make a favorable impression upon the jurors. Dr. Kelly also testified that blackouts generally last no more than four hours and do not remove a person's ability to assess situations, to be aware of his actions, or to control them so that they conform to the requirements of the law, even if he subsequently may not recall them. As an example, the psychiatrist noted that just before committing the killing the defendant had deliberately parked his rented car where it could not be seen from the cottage. Dr. Kelly, whose voice sounds like Alan Alda's, explained the intricacies of the Minnesota Multiphasic Personality Inventory test, which measures a person's ability to devise and to modify tactics as a means of solving problems. He noted that the defendant possessed "suicidal ideation," and had once made a gesture of shooting himself with an imaginary gun, and he agreed that addiction to mood-altering drugs can engender both suicidal and homicidal thoughts or fantasies; indeed, the Food and Drug Administration, he conceded, now requires that such drugs carry a warning label about possible suicidal side-effects and is looking into homicidal ones. He acknowledged that he hadn't checked the defendant's hands for chafing or excoriation and hadn't asked whether his subject practiced any other compulsive rituals. At one point, the defense attorney, impatient at a long answer, sarcastically inquired, "Are you all set?" That evening, following the conclusion of Dr. Kelly's testimony, I anonymously e-mailed him a link to

Drugstore.com's prescription department. I received no acknowledgment. Dr. Richard Neufeld, the defendant's general-care physician, who had written prescriptions for many of his tranquilizers and anti-anxiety drugs, briefly testified that Mr. Toolan never confided his legal or psychiatric problems. This doctor, who joked that his handwriting was supposed to be illegible because he was a physician, was only one of several whom the defendant used in a compartmentalized way to obtain mood- altering medications. A Nantucket police officer testified that Ms. Lochtefeld had spoken with him about obtaining a restraining order against Mr. Toolan but had never actually applied for one. During the ensuing break, I mentioned to Mr. Reddington that Drugstore.com does sell prescription drugs, noting that at least one local pharmacy sometimes orders from that company becase its retail prices are lower than those of the traditional wholesalers. The defendant's father overheard this conversation and looked at me with an expression of interest and faint hope. Not for the first time I pitied him. Lieutenant Jerry Adams, the island's chief of detectives, also overheard and glanced at me quizzically. To remove any misapprehension, I approached him and repeated what I'd said, and this seemed to satisfy him. I even asked him apologetically whether he is often kidded about having the same name (though with different orthography) as the head of the Irish Republican Army, and he smilingly replied, "All the time. I get a lot of free beer in Boston." A few minutes later I encountered the defense attorney sitting on a bench on Center Street, and he greeted me cordially. I asked whether he still felt that the trial was "flirting with being a hollow formality," and he answered, "No, I have a good feeling about this jury." Of course: what else would he say? The pained expression in his eyes seemed to reflect not the banality of my question but his real thoughts about the probable outcome. I had mentioned my communications with Mr. Reddington to a staff photographer sitting next to me during the trial sessions, and he inquired, "What moves [read 'possesses'] you to do this?" I replied, "Sympathy for the underdog; the sense that, notwithstanding the horrible nature of the defendant's crime, to lock him up and throw away the key seems too extreme." But I still cannot imagine Mr. Toolan resuming a productive role in society or not posing a danger to himself and to others. And, although the defense presentation has not yet begun, I think that the likeliest verdict is a finding of guilty of first- degree murder. According to the staff photographer, such a verdict would leave the judge with no choice but to impose a sentence of life imprisonment without the possibility of parole; apparently, the discretion to reduce the verdict to second-degree murder, reportedly exercised over a score of years ago by the judge presiding over the previous murder trial on the island, is no longer a judicial option, and would in any event be unlikely to be invoked in this case, which has inspired local residents to wish aloud for the reenactment of a death-penalty statute. If the judge does indeed sentence the defendant to life imprisonment without parole, what a waste that will be of yet another life destroyed by demon rum — or, in this case, vodka. Ironically, the trial is taking place in a location in which prosecutions and convictions for driving under the influence are all too common; not long ago, even the fire chief was so charged and, among other things, obliged to resign. Over the weekend I read Brian McDonald's *Safe Harbor: A Murder In Nantucket . It describes some disturbing* behavior by the defendant: surprising elderly people on the street and threatening with a hissing voice to give them the back of his hand; strangling almost to death a former girlfriend in the wee hours after finding in her purse a business card belonging to one of her former boyfriends; twice urinating on terrified women whom he didn't know but who had inadvertently annoyed him. Even if some of these stories are apocryphal, as at least one of the press representatives covering the trial believes that collectively they support McDonald's characterization of Mr. Toolan as possessed by a pathological hatred of women. Before the eleventh day of the trial began on the following Monday, there was a brief session of the district court featuring mostly a motley assortment of persons arrested during the previous weekend for disorderly conduct, i.e., public drunkenness. At least one chap appeared in handcuffs. For him and some others, Lieutenant Adams expressed willingness to dismiss the charges upon payment of court costs at the apparent tourist rate of two hundred dollars per miscreant. The handcuffed fellow whom I saw was reminded by the judge that he faced hearings in Cambridge this month and in Roxbury the following month. This seemed to be another case of a chronic offender descending the slippery slope. The defendant's mother was the first witness on the eleventh day of the trial. Hard of hearing even with an aid, Mrs. Toolan testified about her son's history of alcoholism beginning at age twelve, drug abuse including smoking marijuana and snorting cocaine that began at age thirteen, his treatment in rehabilitation facilities, and psychiatric counseling, as well as his work stints in Atlanta, Santa Fe, New York, and Nantucket, where in the early nineties he worked and acted at the Actors' Theater. She remembered that at age seven or eight "Tommy" had injured his head and been x-rayed by a Brooklyn doctor. She noted that by junior year of high school — a year after winning a New York State Regents' commendation for his studiousness — her son towered above his classmates, and that his height and deep voice helped him gain admission to bars and taverns, and that when he began to drink he lost interest in his school work, was diagnosed with attention deficit order, and instead of studying began to listen to music "all the time." She said that she and her husband had discovered some marijuana in their apartment during their son's senior year and arranged for him to see a psychiatrist. At age eighteen or nineteen, she said, he had attempted suicide and after the failed attempt told his parents that he wished he were dead. She noted that he attended four universities and after six years finally earned a baccalaureate at Columbia. She testified that the defendant obtained drugs both legally from pharmacies on Broadway in Manhattan and illegally from websites in Miami and Europe. She described his disheveled appearance, swollen tongue, and slurred speech on the Saturday morning that preceded the killing two days later. She recounted his despair at having his marriage proposal rejected by Ms. Lochtefeld on Friday afternoon at the Metropolitan Museum of New York, where he had even proffered a $1,500 diamond-and-ruby engagement ring. Instead of accepting it, the victim spoke of a sculptor whom she had dated in Nantucket. "During a courtroom break," wrote Cynthia Fagen of *The New York Post*, "the teary mom went over to Lochtefeld's stoic mother and the two comforted each other, clasping hands for several minutes." The next witness was Dr. Ronald Ebert, a forensic neuropsychologist who had taught at Harvard Medical School and had testified before Congress about the U.S. Iowa investigation. Dr. Ebert acknowledged that in the vast majority of the two hundred cases in which he has testified he has done so for the defense. After reviewing the records, he interviewed the defendant four times, each session lasting at least two and one-half hours. The first such meeting was at the Barnstable House of Corrections, where Mr. Toolan paranoiacally and baselessly believed that the officers were listening and yelled disparaging remarks at them through an intercom. The next three conversations took place in a room at the Barnstable courthouse. Dr. Ebert found the defendant intense, anxious, suspicious, obsessed with his appearance to the point of polishing his fingernails, but cooperative. He noted that Mr. Toolan had discharged himself from the Silver Hill, Connecticut rehabilitation facility after a single day against medical advice. He gave the defendant another Minnesota Multiphasic Personality Inventory and studied the results of a depression inventory test that had been administered at the Hazelton, Minnesota facility during the first stay there in 1999 and that showed low self-esteem covered by a veneer of easy social interaction. At that time, he said, the diagnosis was chemical dependency plus an anxiety disorder. By his second stay in 2001, Mr. Toolan also suffered from a major depressive disorder with moderate recurrence. This qualified as a major mental illness. The defendant's addictions to anti-depressants (including the pills intended for his dog during thunderstorms), anti-anxiety medications, and alcohol were recited. His compulsive checking of doorknobs and light switches was noted. Dr. Ebert testified that he referred Mr. Toolan to a Dr. Davidoff at the same Harvard-affiliated hospital where he himself practiced, and that the results of Dr. Davidoff's neuro-psychological testing over an eight-hour period showed that the defendant had suffered alcohol-and- drug-abuse-caused brain damage to the frontal lobes, which process data and house impulse control; such damage, he said, not visible in CT-scans or magnetic resonance imaging, can become dramatic over time as drinking continues. Blackouts and memory loss in the early stages can progress to speech difficulties and even dementia as continued alcoholism further damages the frontal lobes in a vicious cycle. Mr. Toolan's blackouts typically lasted a day or more; this implicitly contradicted Dr. Kelly's testimony that such blackouts rarely last more than four hours, and the doctor also dismissed Dr. Kelly's reliance on simple tests of number and color recognition as superficial and inadequate. Dr. Ebert said that the damage to the defendant's frontal lobes affects his behavior when he is stressed or intoxicated. Dr. Ebert then testified to the following: The effect of Mr. Toolan's blackout on the weekend before the killing was that his memory did not record his trip to the airport, his passing out and missing his flight (testified to by a Continental Airlines pilot boarding that flight as a passenger returning home to Nantucket, who referred to the defendant as "Sleeping Beauty"), or the killing itself. He had traces of recollection of the discovery of the knife at LaGuardia Airport, of offering a reward for that discovery, and of throwing something away in the bushes on the Boulevard in Nantucket en route to the airport and something else at the airport. He remembered crying and being drunk and angry when Ms. Lochtefeld broke up with him on Friday. If these statements are true, then his statement to the Rhode Island police that he hadn't "seen Beth since Friday" may have been his actual recollection and not a dissembling. He didn't recall being rescued on the roof of the New York Athletic Club or the subsequent Alcoholics Anonymous meeting but did recollect trying to buy vodka as well as the fact that the knife he tried to smuggle aboard the flight to Nantucket came from his apartment. He remembered receiving a cell phone message from his therapist that he had missed an appointment; he remembered being arrested. In Dr. Ebert's professional opinion, Mr. Toolan appreciated the wrongfulness of his actions but was incapable of conforming his conduct to the requirements of the law, so he cannot be held legally responsible for his lethal actions. Once he embarked upon those actions, his "persevering quality" prevented him from stopping. The doctor said the defendant understands that his substance abuse has hurt himself and his parents but does not comprehend fully how it has destroyed his life, and that the doctor added that the defendant *chose [emphasis added] to continue* drinking after the first stay at Hazelton. The doctor further testified about the defendant's history of shoplifting and his pleasure in "getting away with stuff." Dr. Ebert agreed with the prosecutor that Mr. Toolan's elaborate planning of the killing demonstrated mental competence. And blackouts in themselves, the witness testified, do not absolve the person who suffers from them of responsibility for his actions. When the prosecutor commented, "It's obvious that you're not a physician, right?" he replied, "That's very obvious." His testimony, he said, conformed to psychological, not medical, certainty. He mentioned, too, an investigation into Mr. Toolan during his ongoing incarceration; the judge instructed the jury not to speculate on the cause of this investigation but indicated he would apprise them of its nature once they had returned a verdict. The final witness on this day was Dr. David Benjamin, a short but scrappy pharmacologist and toxicologist who identified himself as an expert in these areas, but then, after being advised by the judge in consequence of an objection by the prosecutor that he couldn't call himself an expert, then described himself as "a very learned person." The judge accepted this and directed him to proceed. Dr. Benjamin testified that he had worked for the Food and Drug Administration on drug approvals. He described with scientific but not medical certainty the absorption, distribution, and metabolization of alcohol through the blood, and the subsequent conversion in the kidneys and excretion through urination. He calculated a retrograde extrapolation of Mr. Toolan's blood alcohol level at noon on October 25, six hours before it was tested at .0185 in Rhode Island, as anywhere between .03 and .042, depending upon the defendant's ability to metabolize alcohol, and indicated that for a chronic and heavy drinker such as the defendant the higher level was the more likely. He said that comas commence at a blood alcohol level of 0.45 and death above 0.5. A drug taken by Mr. Toolan called Antibase makes one sick if one ingests potable alcohol or even if one applies topical after-shave lotion containing non-potable alcohol. The defendant, the doctor testified, was taking prescription medications for agitation and psychosis as well as to control stomach acid, and also ingesting tranquilizers in the class of Valium and Librium as a means of suppressing the desire to drink alcoholic beverages. Such drugs in the benzodiazepine class depress the central nervous system, have soporific or sedative effects, and are addictive. At one point Dr. Benjamin asked to look at the chart, then held by the prosecutor, in order to answer a question. "Are you familiar with the chart, Doctor?" "There's a lot of material in that chart, sir." Although these physicians seemed more knowledgeable and spent more time with the defendant than Dr. Kelly, they still relied on Mr. Toolan's own account of what he remembered and didn't recall, and they conceded that the defendant *chose [emphasis added] to* continue to drink or to resume drinking and drugging at critical junctures after admissions to rehabilitation facilities and after attendance at Alcoholics Anonymous meetings. They did not deny Mr. Toolan's responsibility for his actions even though he was aware of their wrongfulness because they thought him incapable of stopping short of carrying them through. These findings are in accordance with the dictates of common sense and seem unlikely, in my opinion, to mitigate the jury's probable verdict. This time, the defendant's parents' money may not bail him out of his difficulties. On the first day of October, another murder trial is scheduled to commence in Cambridge, Massachusetts: the Commonwealth vs. Neil Entwistle for the alleged fatal shooting of his wife and daughter. Mr. Entwistle is being represented by Elliot M. Weinstein, a member of the public defender's office. One wonders whether Attorney Weinstein's budget will cover retainers to Harvard psychiatrists and criminologists. Before the twelfth day of the trial got underway, I asked members of the media if they knew the nature and timing of the prison investigation of the defendant that had been mentioned the previous day. I learned that an unimpeachable source had confided in one of them, who told others, three of whom informed me, that more than a year ago Mr. Toolan was suspected of conspiring with at least one other prisoner to escape. A note to this effect — perhaps planted there by another inmate seeking to "frame" him — was found in his cell. Whether additional charges were filed or are pending was not mentioned. Perhaps this alleged incident is what caused the defendant to be kept in solitary confinement in recent months, as his friend Mark Mitchell reported, and also to be concerned that the guards were spying upon him during interviews with psychologists and psychiatrists, with the reported intention of notifying NBC of their discoveries. The twelfth day commenced with the judge defining "indifferent" as "impartial" and "open-minded," and confirming that the jurors continued to exhibit these attributes. The first witness was Dr. Donald Davidoff, a clinical neuropsychologist with degrees from the City University of New York and the Massachusetts Institute of Technology, and also an assistant professor at Harvard Medical School with full privileges at its affiliated hospital in Belmont. His expertise, he testified, is in the fields of dementia, depression, and neurosis, and he has published several monographs and abstracts upon these subjects in learned journals. He has previously testified in Massachusetts on at least fifty occasions. He brought with him a model of a brain and, apparently unintentionally, left it in the courtroom after his testimony. Studies of standardized testing on World War II veterans with head wounds established, he said, a correlation between the integrity of the brain and behavior. A lesion in any part of the brain will cause damage. By standardized he meant measuring an individual against peers in age, sex, and education. Speech and language, he explained, are controlled by the area of the brain behind the frontal lobes; executive function, by the area in front of the frontal lobes. After studying the defendant's history from available records, he described Mr. Toolan's bizarre behavior such as placing two napkins under his wrists before a meal and then wrapping a third napkin around a sandwich so as not to touch it with his fingers while eating it, or his concern that the warden out of spite would place an unclean street person in the second bed in his cell. The witness spoke of the defendant's blackouts with traces of recollections, or what a layman would term selective memory. In a room in the Barnstable courthouse, at Mr. Toolan's insistence and with the permission of prison authorities, he described the defendant's obsessive-compulsive behavior such as frequent hand washing and touching of things in order to prevent terrible things from happening to him. At age seven, for example, Mr. Toolan repeatedly touched a scar on his arm in order to prevent it from becoming infected and falling off. He testified that Mr. Toolan was not malingering or feigning dementia but rather made a sincere effort to cooperate and tell the truth. In other words, although the accounts of the defendant's blackouts came from his own mouth, they were clinically validated, i.e., given professional credence. He administered simple tests that he described to the defendant as difficult, as well as other, more subtle tests that seemed to reveal a pattern of correct answers but actually required different responses, somewhat like the theater of the absurd dramatized in *The Zoo Story* and other plays by Edward Albee. On some of these tests even a patient suffering from Alzheimer's disease can score six out of fifteen correct answers, so if Mr. Toolan had dissembled to appear sicker than he was it would have been evident. The dizziness and fainting spells reported by the defendant coincided with periods of substance abuse. When the prosecutor asked whether the complex planning that led up to the killing didn't indicate competent executive functioning on the part of the defendant, the witness replied, "Cognitive function is not an on-off switch" — a phrase he repeated more than once. Mr. Toolan's ability to recognize changes in the patterns of correct answers was substandard, the neuropsychologist testified, because of damage caused by drinking and drugging to his left frontal cortex, the seat of problem-solving. He was perseverative, i.e., not readily able to learn from a series of answers that the therapist said were incorrect, and not sufficiently flexible to change his tactics quickly. Once embarked upon a course, he had difficulty in modifying it. Other tests measured his visual-spatial processing and language skills, and they pointed to frontal-lobe damage and impairment. A magnetic resonance imaging test, the neuropsychologist added, can show only gross lesions, not microscopic damage to nerve fibers. This expert concluded that Mr. Toolan's childhood head injuries coupled with chronic substance abuse caused cortex deficits, rendered him dysfunctional, lessened his inhibitions and impulse control during intervals of emotional arousal, and removed his ability to conform his behavior to the requirements of the law, thus relieving him of responsibility for his allegedly criminal actions. Simply put, he said, the defendant was unable to act in his own best interests. The witness testified that benzodiazepines such as Zoloft have the same physiological effect as alcohol in that they depress the central nervous system, making one appear drunk and uninhibited, and causing agitation and suicidal ideation. Clonazepam also causes homicidal ideation. Upon cross-examination, the witness admitted not viewing the video of the defendant taken in Rhode Island or some other records but insisted that they were not essential to his diagnosis. Nor did his examination cover Mr. Toolan's condition on October 25, 2004, but he said the defendant's frontal-lobe damage definitely existed on that date. In general, he added, Mr. Toolan's cognitive deficits affected his relationships with colleagues as well as significant others. The defendant had told him about one admission to a rehabilitation center when in fact there were three such admissions. The witness conceded that Mr. Toolan *chose [emphasis added] to drink* after each discharge, and admitted that he hadn't known about the defendant's therapist, who, it developed, was only a social worker, not a psychologist or a psychiatrist. This therapist had insisted that Mr. Toolan regularly snorted cocaine even though he denied doing so at the Silver Hill facility in Connecticut. This misstatement, he said, was an error, not a lie. Although the defendant avoids messy and dirty places, his own apartment exhibited these qualities, but the superintendent never felt the need to call the health department or — in reference to the white German shepherd — the animal rescue service. It is organic brain damage that causes blackouts, not the reverse. The witness conceded that Mr. Toolan controlled his impulse to jump off the roof of the New York Athletic Club, and testified that the defendant was intrigued by illegal exploits. He noted that Mr. Toolan had three complete psychiatric evaluations over an eight-year period, more than most people receive in a lifetime, and that these tests validated the defendant's claims of blackouts, which, again, were caused by organic brain damage. After the "incident" at Ms. Lochtefeld's house, the defendant retained sufficient executive function to change his shirt and coat, the witness conceded to the prosecutor. But his outfit, replete with a feathered hat, sunglasses, and scarf, and stained with blood, the defense attorney elicited upon redirect examination, was garish and stuck out like a sore thumb, serving more to call attention to himself than to act as a disguise. Dr. Anthony Joseph, a neuropsychiatrist, was the next witness called by the defense. A board-certified specialist in geriatric psychiatry, Dr. Joseph also teaches at Harvard Medical School, has consulted for attorneys general in several states, and is an expert in brain imaging and in the neuro- anatomy of psychiatric disturbances. After reviewing what he (although not necessarily the prosecutor) considered to be all of the relevant records, including testimonies before the grand jury that returned the indictment against Mr. Toolan, this doctor had performed an evaluation of the defendant during the course of two interviews and catalogued his ailments as including mild hypomania or bipolar disorder, formerly called manic-depressive disease; paranoia and psychosis; aggressiveness, disinhibition, and impaired insight and impulse control or self-control generally; difficulty turning his attention from an obsession to normal matters. Each deficit alone, or several combined, were capable of making the defendant unable to conform his conduct to the requirements of the law. Upon cross-examination, the prosecutor won from this psychiatrist a concession that Mr. Toolan could have been sober during the "incident" and become drunk thereafter. This line of reasoning, however, may prove a double-edged sword: does Mr. Glenny unintentionally imply that if the defendant were drunk during the killing it would absolve him of criminal responsibility, or at least diminish that responsibility? The doctor conceded that Mr. Toolan hadn't fought with his friend Mark Mitchell when pulled back from the roof, thus exhibiting self-control at that moment. Had he jumped, of course, there would be no trial taking place. This physician had ordered a magnetic resonance imaging test, which proved normal, but he testified that in the early stages of dementia there would be no visible brain damage. The defendant procured muscle relaxant from Tijuana, it was disclosed, and claimed that he saw alligators and dogs during morning-after hangovers. But Mr. Glenny contended that the defendant was just making up stories to deceive the doctors, noting that even the tale about the dog needing tranquilizers during thunderstorms came from Mr. Toolan alone, not from any veterinarian's records. The prosecutor ridiculed the notion that the defendant suffered a blackout lasting from the time he left the bar in New York until his arrest in Rhode Island, eliciting an admission that during this entire time the defendant was able to drive without causing a single accident. But the doctor insisted that Mr. Toolan's ability to remember some details during that time does not mean that no lengthy blackout occurred. Such a blackout may not be total at a given moment, but the defendant could and did have a high degree of memory impairment during that twenty-four hour period. Moreover, the psychiatrist asserted, the alleged blackout was only one element considered in his evaluation of Mr. Toolan's criminal responsibility for the "incident." He alluded to the peripheral or anecdotal evidence of the Force 5 clerk's saying that the defendant "freaked me out" to show that Mr. Toolan was deeply psychotic at that time, and pointed again to other, more clinical evidence of such a psychosis. "If one is addicted," asked the prosecutor, "can one choose to resume drinking?" The doctor hedged, then answered affirmatively in view of the defendant's year-long period of sobriety. The prosecutor, concluding his questioning, effectively had the last word: the defense rested. Tomorrow the closing arguments and judge's instructions to the jury are expected to last until one-thirty in the afternoon. Then the case will be remanded to the jury for its deliberation upon a verdict. Will the jury heed the testimony of the Harvard-educated professionals, or will it apply common sense and conclude that alcoholism is essentially voluntary and does not relieve the defendant of responsibility for his allegedly criminal actions? Determinism or free will? If I were a betting man, I'd wager on the latter outcome, especially in the venue of Nantucket. But time will tell — and not much time at that, if one interprets the judge's advice to the jurors that they would not be permitted to leave the building during their deliberations to signify that he expects a verdict by late afternoon tomorrow. But that is probably not his Honor's meaning, and jurors may be reluctant to sentence a man to life imprisonment after only brief deliberation. Author Brian McDonald was in attendance on Day Thirteen of the trial, he and responded in the negative when I asked him whether he planned to write a book about the trial. The day's commenced with the judge providing general instructions to the jury, and his performance was very mpressive. He admonished jurors not to attribute heightened credibility to those whom he termed "so-called expert witnesses," who are, after all, only human, or to be intimidated by them, but rather to apply their common sense and accumulated experience in deciding whether to believe all, part, or none of any such witness' testimony about "facts" or hypotheticals. After the closing arguments, he indicated, he will provide specific instructions on the law, including the definitions of first-degree or premeditated murder with malice aforethought, second-degree murder with a lesser degree of premeditation, and voluntary manslaughter with no malice, and the degrees of intent inherent in each relative to the defendant's history of intoxication and mental defects. He said he will also discuss the consequences of a verdict of not guilty by reason of insanity, i.e., commitment to a mental hospital for the criminally insane. He reminded the jurors that they must return a verdict not only on the murder charge but also on the charge of assault and battery by means of a dangerous weapon with extreme atrocity and cruelty. He noted that some jurors were taking notes and did not proscribe them from doing so but said that they would receive written copies of his ongoing instructions. He warned jurors not to speculate or to guess about "real" facts not introduced into evidence, to ignore any promised evidence not presented in court, and not to allow sympathy for or impressions of any of the parties involved to color their decision, which must be based solely on the evidence of witness testimonies and exhibits: "Sympathy has no place in this courtroom or in any courtroom in America." He instructed them to ignore any difference in attorneys' styles of presentation regardless of their related likes and dislikes, to prefer their own recollections to those of the attorneys, and to accept without reservation the law as he defines it: "I am the judge of the law; you are the judge of the facts." He urged them to weigh the evidence as a whole as well as each piece of evidence individually, to listen to each other's arguments with an open mind, and to speak up with their own opinions. He defined the difference between direct and circumstantial evidence by giving an example from his boyhood: if he saw a milkman leaving bottles of fresh milk on the outside windowsill, that was direct evidence; if he awoke and saw such bottles there, that was circumstantial evidence, from which he could reasonably infer that the milkman had visited the property and left the bottles there. He emphasized that the Commonwealth has the burden of proving its case beyond a reasonable doubt. Then attorney Reddington began his closing arguments by sympathizing with the jurors for their patience in sitting quietly for nearly two weeks without being able to ask any questions. He expressed confidence that their attentiveness to the evidence signified that they were doing their best to be as fair "as humanity permits," and that they would serve the interests of justice in accordance with the law as handed down by the judge. "We are," he reminded them, "a society of laws," and jurors pass between the government and the defendant, who has placed his reliance upon his own country as represented by the jurors. To all this and what followed the jurors were without exception indeed very attentive. Then Mr. Reddington attempted the clever ploy of shifting the burden of what the government must prove beyond a reasonable doubt: it must show, he said, not only that Mr. Toolan killed Ms. Lochtefeld intentionally and with malice aforethought, but also that the defendant was not suffering from a mental disease at that time. It is an axiom of logic that one cannot prove a negative; yet here was the defense counsel attempting to cause the prosecution to do exactly that. He noted that the one hundred forty-four exhibits do not include the defendant's brain, i.e., that no one can know what thoughts were processed there just before, during, and after the "incident." The attorney said that the plea of not guilty by reason of insanity was not the "copout" of someone in prison trying to win an acquittal by pretending to be crazy, but rather a reflection of an actual illness going back many years and corroborated by evidence including medical testimony. He said that while Mr. Toolan may look as if he is operating on all cylinders, in fact he is not doing so, and he is therefore incapable of conforming his conduct to the requirements of the law; that the defendant may look like a master of the universe, but that that is only a mask: Mr. Toolan required six years to earn his baccalaureate and in the process was "discharged," i.e., expelled, by more than one institution of higher learning. Far from being a "big shot," the defense attorney reminded jurors, the defendant worked as a car salesman in Atlanta, as an actor in Nantucket, and subsequently as a bond salesman in the financial industry, where he was fired from several positions, in one case showing up for work one morning only to be asked to leave because of events of the preceding evening [nearly starting a fight at an office party for representatives of competing firms] of which he retained no memory whatsoever by reason of his intoxication from alcohol and drugs. Mr. Toolan, recalled his attorney, had even been foolish enough to attempt to steal a two foot-high statue of Julius Caesar weighing sixty pounds from a serious antiques show by placing it under his jacket as a lark. It was analogous, the attorney declared, to his trying to place a fifteen-inch computer monitor in use in the courtroom under his coat and walking out with it. The defendant's office was described by Mr. Reddington as essentially devoid of any real work materials, yet the defendant attempted to impress Ms. Lochtefeld by taking her to California and by there attending "important" business meetings to which he carried a Blackberry. It was all a fake, as a fraud who lacked any real self- esteem but strutted as proudly as a peacock with no firm basis for doing so. Mr. Toolan, the attorney reminded the jury once again, suffered from a major depressive disorder caused by drugs, including alcohol: "Alcohol is a drug." He stressed the legitimacy of the medical tests undergone by the defendant, noting that not only were they subjected to peer reviews but that even Dr. Kelly (who had testified on behalf of the district attorney's office) accepted their validity. He reminded them that his client's depression had intensified from 1999 to 2001, and that his hallucinations about alligators and dogs occurred only when he suffered delirium tremens caused by intoxication. He catalogued the mood- controlling drugs ingested by Mr. Toolan in 2001 and the following year, and asked rhetorically where was the bottle of ninety benzodiazepine pills obtained by the defendant just before Labor Day weekend in 2004 with apparent illegality through the website of a company operating in Florida: not in the apartment, not on the defendant's person, hence evidently ingested. He repeated that Mr. Toolan's apartment was a dump that had never been visited by his parents until after the "incident." He reminded jurors that Ms. Lochtefeld had asked a friend from San Diego to be her maid of honor, and stated that her subsequent change of heart and rejection of the defendant's proposal of marriage threw him into an abyss of stupefaction. Attorney Reddington conceded that Mr. Toolan hadn't actually jumped off the roof of the New York Athletic Club — there would probably be no trial if he had — but he insisted that the thought of jumping was present in his diseased mind. **MACBETH :** Canst thou not minister to a mind diseased, Pluck from the memory a rooted sorrow, Raze out the written troubles of the brain And with some sweet oblivious antidote Cleanse the stuff'd bosom of that perilous stuff Which weighs upon the heart? **DOCTOR :** Therein the patient Must minister to himself. Unfortunately the defendant was unable to do so successfully. The attorney, continuing, declared that "any idiot" knows that he can't sneak a ten-inch knife through an airport metal detector. But, in fact, lots of people try, and many knives are confiscated at airports' security stations. Mr. Reddington described his client as not obviously intoxicated during the morning and early afternoon hours of October 25: "Otherwise no one would have sold him knives or rented him cars." Mr. Toolan's voice as recorded in the police cruiser in Rhode Island sounded, the attorney noted, slow but normal. He said his own perennial antagonist, Dr. Kelly, apparently but incorrectly regarding the government's case as overwhelming, had asked the defendant nothing relevant, consulted few records, done no sophisticated testing, performed no investigation before arriving at his usual diagnosis of antisocial disorder, and said only what he thought the government wished to hear. Dr. Kelly, he claimed, would have found nothing wrong with Hannibal Lecter. Dr. Kelly testified that the defendant's magnetic resonance imaging test showed normal results, whereas in previous trials [clearly not in evidence in this one] he had said that "he doesn't do MRI's." In any event, Mr. Reddington reminded jurors, other experts' testimony proved that such scans show only gross, not subtle deformities in the brain. In conclusion, Mr. Reddington asked jurors rhetorically, "Has the government proven beyond a reasonable doubt that the defendant was not insane?" And he asked them to judge the facts in accordance with the law as handed down by his Honor and to render a "true" verdict, based on those facts, of not guilty by reason of insanity caused by a mental disease. The judge then asked jurors if they needed a break or could continue for another forty-five minutes: "This is your first vote," he joked. The jury asked for a break. During the break, representatives of the media flocked around the defense attorney outside the building, as they habitually did during the trial. I never saw a similar gathering around the prosecutor. Assistant District Attorney Brian Glenny then hit the expected high points of his contention that the defendant was sane, comparatively sober, capable of planning and executing a complex plan of premeditated murder, accountable for his conscious choices, aware of the illegality of his actions, and able when he saw fit to conform his conduct to the requirements of the law. "He wanted to kill her. He planned to kill her. And he didn't want to get caught. He knew what he planned to do, and eventually did, was wrong." Mr. Glenny reviewed the expert witnesses' testimonies, attempted to rehabilitate Dr. Kelly once more, and demanded a common-sense verdict of guilty of premeditated first-degree murder with malice aforethought and of assault and battery by means of a dangerous weapon with extreme atrocity and cruelty. Again I quote with permission Hilary Russ' account in the online version of *The Cape Cod Times* : "Many people suffer alcohol or drug addiction, countered Cape and Islands First Assistant District Attorney Brian Glenny, as he began his closing argument. 'The fact that they abuse alcohol or drugs is not an excuse to commit murder,' the prosecutor said. That Mr. Toolan followed Ms. Lochtefeld from room to room 'to complete his murderous task' was proof of 'goal- directed, contemplative planning,' he said." As promised, Judge Connon then instructed the jury on the specific application of the law to the charges in this matter. To arrive at a guilty verdict, he said, the jury must find that the prosecution had proven the charges beyond a reasonable doubt. He defined insanity and summarized the possible verdicts once more and outlined the related sentences. A finding of guilty of first-degree murder, he said, would subject the defendant to a sentence of life imprisonment without any possibility of parole but trigger an automatic appeal; of second-degree murder, to a sentence of life imprisonment with a possibility of parole; of voluntary manslaughter, to a sentence of a shorter prison term; of acquittal, to commitment to a state mental hospital, probably Bridgewater State Hospital. He noted that intoxication by itself is not a valid reason for the jury to render a verdict of not guilty by reason of insanity, but that intoxication could "activate" a mental disorder and lead to that finding — unless jurors decide that Toolan knew that alcohol or drugs would spark a mental disease. He then turned the case over to the jurors for their due deliberation, which continued for ninety minutes, until 4 P.M. After resuming their deliberations at nine o'clock on the morning of the fourteenth day of the trial, June 21, 2007, the jurors rendered their verdict just before noon and about two hours before the official start of summer. Here is reporter Jason Graziadei's account from *The Nantucket Inquirer and Mirror* : "Twelve jurors needed only four [and one-half] hours to decide that Thomas Toolan III was guilty of first-degree murder." Toolan was brought into court handcuffed for the verdict. He had not been handcuffed throughout the trial. He left the courtroom in ankle shackles after the sentencing. The former Manhattan bank executive was immediately sentenced to life in prison without parole for the killing of his ex-girlfriend, Elizabeth "Beth" Lochtefeld, in 200 He left Nantucket Superior Court Thursday afternoon in handcuffs and shackles and after a day or two of psychiatric evaluation was transported to the Cedar Junction state prison in Walpole, Massachusetts. After proving to be a model prisoner, he was eventually transferred to another state prison in Shirley, Massachusetts, where he is being held in medium security. Rejecting defense attorney Kevin Reddington's argument that Toolan was insane at the time of the murder, jurors said they found no evidence of a mental disease or defect, and decided that the killing was a premeditated act of a man who knew what he was doing and understood the consequences. Mr. Reddington himself while insisting that all the evidence to justify an acquittal had been presented, later acknowledged that the verdict was "what the man on the street expected." A tense courtroom had waited anxiously for the verdict as the jury finished its deliberations just before noon on Thursday. Members of the Lochtefeld family cried and hugged each other after the guilty verdict was announced. Sitting with her husband in the same spot they had occupied throughout the trial, Toolan's mother Dolores also wept when the jury returned its verdict. "It's not a happy day for anyone. We don't rejoice in this," said Tom Lochtefeld, Beth's brother, outside the courthouse. "We find no glee that he'll spend the rest of his life in some hellhole." Catherine Lochtefeld, Beth's sister, read a victim-impact statement on behalf of the family in the courthouse, which her brother Jim read again for the television cameras outside the building. "We can never forget the sorrow brought on by her death, which was sudden, violent, undeserved, and alone. Our grief was sharp, intense, palpable and difficult to bear," Catherine Lochtefeld said. "We do not rejoice that Mr. Toolan's parents have, for all purposes, lost their son, even as Beth's parents have lost their daughter. Yet we are relieved that this troubled, vengeful and dangerous man will never be able to harm another innocent person." After nearly three weeks of listening to testimony and legal arguments, as well as reviewing a mountain of evidence, members of the jury left the courthouse quickly, attempting to avoid the media by exiting the building through a side door. But one juror, Kelly Garrett, said there was no evidence presented that convinced her that Toolan was insane at the time of the murder: "We went through all the medical records with a fine-toothed comb," Garrett said. "There just wasn't evidence of that in the medical records. We looked at the law and we felt he was responsible." Prosecutor Brian Glenny, who methodically proved that Toolan executed a premeditated plan to murder his ex-girlfriend in her Hawthorne Lane cottage nearly three years ago, praised the different law enforcement agencies involved in the investigation as well as the Loctefeld family: "At no time did we ever think that it was a legitimate defense," Glenny said. "We never subscribed to the theory that he was not criminally responsible. The Lochtefelds have gone through a tragic situation. To hear during a two-week trial how your daughter, sister or cousin was murdered is difficult, and they were able to do that in commendable fashion." Asked if he felt Toolan had received a fair trial on Nantucket despite the pretrial publicity and the small community from which the jury was chosen, Glenny said, "Without question." In summary: Toolan was found guilty not only of first-degree murder, which carries a mandatory sentence of life in prison, but also assault and battery with a dangerous weapon. He was also sentenced to nine to ten years in prison on that charge, which will run concurrently with his life sentence. The guilty verdict does, however, trigger an automatic appeal to the state Supreme Judicial Court. Reddington, one of the top defense attorneys in the state, said he would not represent Toolan in the appeal, because "I don't do appeals." Asked for his reaction to the verdict, Reddington said, "You do the math: one hundred forty-four exhibits, two weeks of trial, and a verdict in five hours? I understand it. I don't really feel very pleased about it. But everyone in the courthouse and in the community expected it. "The Toolan family is very distressed," Reddington continued. "They can't understand why more deliberation and consideration weren't put into it. The evidence was there as to the brain defect." The fact that Judge Richard Connon rejected his motion for a change of venue will be central to Toolan's appeal, Reddington said, as well as the fact that a juror was caught dozing on Wednesday during Connon's instructions. In a prepared statement issued after the verdict was read, District Attorney Michael O'Keefe said, "I hope that this brings some measure of peace to the Lochtefeld family. They sat in the courtroom every day listening to some very difficult testimony." O'Keefe also thanked Nantucket police chief William Pittman and his department, as well as state police detectives from the district attorney's office, for their tireless work on the case. Jim Lochtefeld, one of Beth's brothers, continued to read the family's statement outside the courtroom after the verdict was announced. "Speaking on behalf of those who loved Beth, we will always remember the joy and kindness that she brought to those around her. Beth's cup was full of enthusiasm, curiosity, adventure, and laughter; it overflowed with love and forgiveness. Her intelligence and achievements were remarkable," Jim Lochtefeld said. "We have always trusted that her accused killer would come to trial. It is not for us to judge his guilt or innocence. We have come here to stand in Beth's place, conscious that it was only the jurors' judgment that really mattered, and that we would accept it. To that end, we always trusted that justice would be served." Mr. Reddington proved prescient, however, in pinpointing Judge Connon's denial of a change of venue as a principal issue upon automatic appeal. But first, after due deliberation, the judge denied motions for a retrial on various grounds, including that of the allegedly sleeping juror, whom he said he had noticed closing his eyes but not nodding off to sleep. Then, in

August 2013, the Supreme Judicial Court of Massachusetts vacated the conviction because, its justices decided, Judge Connon had not sufficiently shielded the jurors from prejudicial pre-trial publicity in Nantucket. In June 2013, another jury in Barnstable Superior Court again found Mr. Toolan guilty of all charges. Whereas the Nantucket jury had deliberated for a total of four and one-half hours — about as long, wrote Hilary Russ, as it would have taken the defendant to drive from Hyannis to his Manhattan apartment had he not been stopped by state police in Rhode Island — their counterparts in Barnstable required only three hours to render a verdict of guilty as charged. That verdict, too, was subject to an automatic appeal, which after several false starts by other criminal defense attorneys was conducted by Michelle Menken, who filed a brief drawing distinctions between mental defects or deficiencies and other psychiatric ailments, including cognitive impairment. The prosecutor, Elizabeth Anne Sweeny, countered that the Barnstable Superior Court judge, the Honorable Gary A. Nickerson, had given the jury the model instructions, and that no additional instructions pertaining to allegedly disabling psychiatrtic disorders were either necessary or appropriate. And Ms. Menken argued that a "statute" cited by Dr. Kelly did not exist, justifying the SJC to reduce Mr. Toolan's conviction to second- degree murder, for which the statutory penalty is a number of years at the judge's discretion up to life with the possibility of parole. Prosecutor Sweeney, emphasizing that Judge Nickerson had recited the model instructions to the jury, reminded the justices that the defendant's crime met all of the criteria for first-degree murder: Mr. Toolan had traveled from New York City to Nantucket, bought a knife there, and stabbed Ms. Lochtefeld twenty-three times. Oral argument embodying these contentions was held before the full Court on May 4, 2022, and on September 23, 2022, the Supreme Judicial Court of the Commonwealth of Massachusetts affirmed the 2013 Barnstable conviction nearly eighteen years after the murder of Elizabeth Lochtefeld on October 25, 2004. Readers may review the history of the case on the Court's website; the case number is SJC-11589, where there is a link to the oral arguments held on May 4, 2022 on Suffolk University Law School's website.

On September 23, 2022, the SJC issued a "rescript" or transcript of its findings, over the objections of the defense attorney:

Rescript: (Full Opinion): Judgments affirmed(By the Court)

MOTION to stay issuance of the rescript filed

for Thomas E. Toolan, III by Attorney MichelleMenken.(11/30/2022) The motion is denied.

RESCRIPT ISSUED to trial court.

TOOLAN, COMMONWEALTH vs., 490 Mass. 698 (masscases.com)

COMMONWEALTH vs. THOMAS E. TOOLAN, THIRD.

490 Mass. 698

May 4, 2022 - September 23, 2022

Court Below: Superior Court, Nantucket County

Present: Budd, C.J., Lowy, Cypher, Kafker, & Georges, JJ.

Records And Briefs:

- (1) SJC-11589 01 Appellant Toolan Brief
- (2) SJC-11589 03 Appellee Commonwealth Brief
- (3) SJC-11589 04 Appellant Toolan Reply Brief

SJC-11589

Homicide. Assault and Battery by Means of a Dangerous Weapon. Drug Addiction. Criminal Responsibility. Mental Impairment. Malice. Intoxication. Practice, Criminal, Capital case, Instructions to jury, Request for jury instructions. Words, "Mental disease or defect."

At a murder trial, the brief testimony from an expert witness for the Commonwealth concerning the legal definition of a mental disease or defect did not give rise to a substantial likelihood of a miscarriage of justice. [705-707]

At a murder trial, no prejudicial error arose from the judge's decision not to provide the jury with a supplemental instruction, requested by the defendant, distinguishing between a lack of criminal responsibility and diminished capacity, where the judge had defined both terms in language consistent with the Model Jury Instructions on Homicide. [707-710]

At the trial of indictments charging murder and assault and battery by means of a dangerous weapon, the judge did not err in instructing the jury that they could, but need not, infer an intent to kill from the intentional use of a dangerous weapon in the circumstances of the case, where the instruction essentially quoted the then applicable Model Jury Instructions on Homicide, and where the evidence of malice was overwhelming. [710-713]

At a murder trial, no substantial likelihood of a miscarriage of justice arose from the lack of an instruction to the jury that they should consider whether the defendant was incapable of resisting the urge to consume drugs or alcohol, where the judge properly instructed the jury that they could determine the defendant's degree of criminal responsibility by considering his mental disease or defect and its interaction with his consumption of drugs and alcohol, and where there was ample evidence before the jury to support a finding that the defendant's conduct was knowing and intentional and undertaken after substantial planning, notwithstanding his evident intoxication at the time of the attack. [713-716]

Indictments found and returned in the Superior Court Department on January 10, 2005.

Following review by this court, 460 Mass. 452 (2011), the cases were tried before Gary A. Nickerson, J.

Michelle Menken for the defendant.

Elizabeth A. Sweeney, Assistant District Attorney, for the Commonwealth.

GEORGES, J. This case is before the court on the defendant's direct appeal from his convictions of murder in the first degree and assault and battery by means of a dangerous weapon in the stabbing death of Elizabeth Locktefeld, his former girlfriend, on October 25, 2004. Locktefeld was found dead on the floor of her home in Nantucket, having been stabbed twenty-three times, a few days after she ended her relationship with the defendant due to what she described as his excessive consumption of alcohol.

In this appeal, the defendant raises a number of challenges to the jury instructions given and the absence of requested instructions. He maintains that the judge should have clarified the legal definition of "mental disease or defect" after the Commonwealth's expert testified inappropriately by referencing a statutory definition, and that the absence of a clarifying instruction created a substantial likelihood of a miscarriage of justice. The defendant argues also that the judge's instructions did not adequately explain the difference between a lack of criminal responsibility and diminished capacity, such that the jury might not have understood that, if they found the defendant had been criminally responsible, they nonetheless could find the defendant had had a diminished capacity at the time of the stabbing. In addition, the defendant contends that it was error to instruct the jury that they could infer malice from the intentional use of a dangerous weapon. The defendant also maintains that the judge abused his discretion in not instructing the jury, as the defendant requested, to consider whether the defendant was incapable of resisting the urge to use drugs or alcohol, and thus that any knowledge the defendant might have had about the effect of intoxication upon his mental conditions should not have been considered in the determination whether the defendant had had a mental impairment at the time. Finally, the defendant asks us to exercise our extraordinary authority to grant him relief under G. L. c. 278, § 33E.

Having carefully reviewed the arguments and the record, we discern no error warranting a new trial and no reason to exercise our extraordinary authority under G. L. c. 278, § 33E, to order a new trial or to reduce the degree of guilt. Accordingly, we affirm the convictions.

1. Background. a. Facts. The jury could have found the following. In the fall of 2004, the defendant was living in New York City, where he had grown up, and the victim was living in

Page 700

Nantucket, where she had moved from New York earlier that year. On September 4, 2004, a mutual friend introduced the defendant and the victim to each other. Shortly thereafter, they began dating; the relationship deepened very quickly, such that the defendant and the victim were discussing marriage. Over the course of a few days in late October of 2004, however, while the victim was visiting the defendant in New York, the relationship degenerated rapidly, due to the defendant's excessive drinking. On around October 23, 2004, the victim ended the relationship for that reason, removed her belongings from the defendant's apartment, and returned to her home in Nantucket.

On October 23, 2004, the defendant called a long-time friend, Mark Mitchell, from a bar. The defendant sounded confused, and his speech was slurred. Mitchell was concerned and went to the bar, where he found the defendant drinking vodka. The defendant went to the rooftop of the building and threatened to commit suicide. Mitchell convinced him to come down from the roof and took the defendant to an Alcoholics Anonymous meeting. After the meeting, the defendant purchased two bottles of vodka from different stores. Mitchell took each bottle from him. Mitchell brought the defendant to the defendant's apartment, and there the defendant fell asleep.

The next day, on October 24, 2004, the defendant went to LaGuardia Airport and purchased a one-way ticket to Nantucket. He was detained while going through security before boarding the plane because he had placed a large kitchen knife in a security bin, along with his coat and carry-on luggage, where it was detected by a scanner. Airport security officials noted that the defendant's breath smelled of alcohol, his eyes were glassy, his speech was slurred, and he appeared to be under the influence of alcohol. When asked about the knife, the defendant gave four differing reasons for having brought it with him. The defendant was issued a summons for possessing a knife with a blade more than four inches in length. He then went to a bar at another terminal.

The following day, October 25, 2004, the defendant returned to LaGuardia Airport and again purchased a ticket to Nantucket. This time, he successfully boarded the plane. When he reached Nantucket, he rented a bright-colored sport utility vehicle (SUV) and drove to a surf shop. He asked a salesperson where the scallop knives were kept. The salesperson told the defendant that the store did not sell any knives, and directed him to a nearby

marine store. There, the defendant purchased two scallop knives and a longer, sheathed knife with an orange handle.

The defendant then drove to the victim's cottage, which was located on the same property as the main house where the landlord lived. He parked across the street, at an angle that partly obstructed passing traffic. He approached the landlord, who was working outside in the yard, and asked whether the victim was home. Although the landlord had just spoken to the victim and had seen her go inside the cottage, the defendant's appearance concerned her, and she replied that she did not know. The defendant headed to the cottage, where the door was standing open and the shades were not drawn. The defendant entered and, during an encounter that left blood on the walls, floor, and furniture in several rooms, stabbed the victim twenty-three times in the torso, chest, back, nose, arms, and hands. Before he left the cottage, the defendant pulled the shades and closed the door. He discarded a beer bottle and a vodka bottle outside the kitchen door. He drove back to the airport, where he left the rental SUV, [Note 1] and flew to Hyannis, where he rented another vehicle and started driving toward New York.

Shortly after the defendant left the cottage, the victim's landlord noticed that the curtains were drawn and the door was shut, contrary to the victim's usual practice. Concerned, the landlord telephoned the victim's brother. The brother called 911 and asked police to conduct a wellness check. After officers found the victim's bloodied body, the brother assisted them in obtaining the defendant's full name and address, and they issued an alert to look for the defendant's rental vehicle. The defendant was located by Rhode Island State police driving on Route 95 in Rhode Island. While troopers were following the defendant's vehicle to an exit where they had set up a roadblock, the defendant drove appropriately, without crossing any marked lanes and without speeding. When he was stopped at the roadblock, the defendant appeared lethargic and bewildered; he was unable to follow officers' commands to unlock the driver's door. The defendant was arrested on suspicion of operating a motor vehicle while under the influence of alcohol and taken to the Hope Valley barracks of the

Rhode Island State police.

Troopers found a prescription bottle of ninety Klonopin tablets in the defendant's vehicle. [Note 2] The prescription had been filled five days earlier, and the bottle contained sixty-two Klonopin pills. The defendant was given a breathalyzer test approximately two hours after his arrest. At that time, the test indicated a blood alcohol level of 0.185.

Troopers from the Massachusetts State police arrived, read the defendant the Miranda warnings, and told him that they were there to discuss the victim. The defendant called a friend and asked the friend to tell the victim to call police and tell them that she was okay. The defendant then continued talking to the officers and said that he had not seen the victim for three days. The clothes the defendant was wearing at the time of his arrest subsequently tested positive for the victim's blood. Officers also searched the defendant's apartment and found "a few" empty bottles of vodka, empty beer bottles, and prescription bottles of Zoloft and Klonopin. [Note 3]

b. Prior proceedings. On January 10, 2005, the defendant was indicted on charges of murder in the first degree, G. L. c. 265, § 1; and assault and battery by means of a dangerous weapon, G. L. c. 265, § 15A. At his first trial in 2007, the Commonwealth proceeded on theories of deliberate premeditation and extreme atrocity or cruelty. The defendant was convicted under both theories.

The defendant appealed on the grounds, inter alia, of improprieties in jury selection and the denial of his motion for a change in venue due to extensive pretrial publicity. In addition, the defendant challenged the instructions on mental defect. See Commonwealth v. DiPadova, 460 Mass. 424, 430-433, 439-440 (2011); Commonwealth v. Berry, 457

Mass. 602, 617-618 & n.9 (2010), S.C., 466 Mass. 763 (2014). He also challenged evidence presented to the jury concerning his exercise of his Miranda rights. We vacated the convictions and ordered a new trial. See Commonwealth v. Toolan, 460 Mass. 452, 472-473 (2011). At his second trial, the defendant relied upon a defense of a lack of criminal responsibility due to mental disease or defect and intoxication. He again was convicted of both charges and under both theories of murder.

2. Discussion. The defendant's arguments on appeal relate to specific jury instructions given or to instructions that were requested but not given; all of the challenged instructions involve issues concerning the defendant's mental state. Jury instructions are evaluated as a whole, and as a reasonable juror would have interpreted them. See Commonwealth v. Odgren, 483 Mass. 41, 46 (2019). A reviewing court presumes that the jury understood and followed the trial judge's instructions. See Commonwealth v. Donahue, 430 Mass. 710, 718 (2000).

At trial, the defense relied upon a theory of a lack of criminal responsibility or diminished capacity. Where a defendant offers a defense of lack of criminal responsibility, the burden rests on the Commonwealth to "prove beyond a reasonable doubt that the defendant was criminally responsible at the time the alleged crime was committed." Commonwealth v. Dunphe, 485 Mass. 871, 878 (2020), quoting Model Jury Instructions on Homicide 1 (2018). The Model Jury Instructions on Homicide provide that a "person is not criminally responsible for his conduct if he has a mental disease or defect, and, as a result of that mental disease or defect, lacks substantial capacity either to appreciate the criminality or wrongfulness of his conduct or to conform his conduct to the requirements of the law." Model Jury Instructions on Homicide 2.

In support of his theory of mental incapacity to have formed the necessary intent, or the existence of a mental impairment, the defendant called three expert witnesses: Dr. Anthony Joseph, a practicing neuropsychiatrist and professor of psychiatry at Harvard Medical School and McLean Hospital; Dr. Donald Davidoff, a neuropsychologist and chief of neuropsychology at McLean Hospital; and Dr. Robert Tittman, a psychiatrist in private practice who also worked at Boston College's counselling service. The Commonwealth called one mental health expert, Dr. Martin Kelly, and also called a physician, Richard Neufeld, who had treated the defendant from 1999 until his arrest in October of 2004. Kelly was a psychiatrist and professor at Harvard Medical School; Neufeld had prescribed the defendant Zoloft, Klonopin, and other medications for mental health conditions. The defendant had been prescribed fifty milligrams of Zoloft daily; that dosage was doubled to one hundred milligrams in late June of 2004.

Joseph, the neuropsychiatrist, opined that, at the time of the stabbing, the defendant had not been legally sane, and had lacked the capacity to conform his conduct to the requirements of the law due to a mental disease or defect. Joseph described the disease or defect as "a number of processes occurring at that time which rendered [the defendant] unable to conform his behavior to the law, and which also caused substantial disorders of memory, perception, thought, and mood." Joseph described the defendant's prior mental health history as including diagnoses of "polysubstance abuse," depression, and psychosis. Joseph also described potential side effects from taking Klonopin and Zoloft, including agitation, mania, and psychosis, and said that an increase in dose made the potential that an individual would experience such side effects more likely.

In addition to conducting a neuropsychiatric interview of the defendant, Davidoff administered a series of standard neuropsychological tests in order to gain an over-all understanding of the defendant's psychological functioning at the time of the interview in 2007. Davidoff offered no opinion with respect to the defendant's criminal responsibility at the time of the stabbing in 2004. Davidoff determined that, when he interviewed the defendant in 2007, the defendant's "executive functions were not operating efficiently," and he was experiencing difficulties with memory, processing "visual information," and being able to remember and use facts "in an efficient, productive way." These problems indicated damage to the frontal lobe, likely from damage due to "chronic alcohol abuse."

Tittmann testified specifically as to the effect of multiple medications, including Zoloft and Klonopin, on the brain, and stated that they could cause confusion, increase the risk of suicide, or aggravate psychosis. He also testified that the use of these

Page 705

substances with others, or with alcohol, would have an "additive or synergistic effect" and would exacerbate the effects of the consumption of alcohol alone. He did not offer an opinion with respect to the defendant's mental state or degree of criminal responsibility at the time of the stabbing.

Kelly, the Commonwealth's psychiatric expert, opined that the defendant suffered from a "personality disorder" with "features of narcissistic personality disorder and antisocial personality disorder." Kelly also opined that the defendant had addictions to alcohol and to benzodiazepines. Kelly did not believe that these mental health issues were a mental disease or defect that would interfere with the defendant's ability to understand the wrongfulness of his conduct or to conform his conduct to the requirements of the law. Kelly pointed to a number of the defendant's actions the day before the stabbing and on the day of the stabbing as indicating an ability to understand wrongfulness; these included hiding a knife in a coat while going through airport security, drawing the curtains at the victim's house, and disposing of items taken from the house before leaving for the mainland.

On cross-examination, Kelly did agree that the defendant previously had attempted suicide and had been committed to psychiatric hospitals on at least three prior occasions with diagnoses of substance abuse disorder and major depressive disorder. Kelly also agreed that, in 2004, the United States Food and Drug Administration had issued warnings about the risks of increased suicidal behavior, as well as the potential for triggering manic episodes, in individuals taking Zoloft, either at the beginning of treatment or when the dosage was increased.

a. *Instruction on mental disease or defect.* The defendant contends that the judge should have clarified the legal meaning of "mental disease or defect" after Kelly gave both a legal definition and then, after objection by defense counsel and instruction by the judge, his professional, clinical definition of that term. As the defendant did not object at trial to the definition of "mental disease or defect" the jury were provided, we review for a substantial likelihood of a miscarriage of justice. See Commonwealth v. Niemic, 427 Mass. 718, 720 (1998), S.C., 451 Mass. 1008 (2008).

Under Commonwealth v. McHoul, 352 Mass. 544, 546-547 (1967), a lack of criminal responsibility is defined as follows:

"A person is not responsible for criminal conduct if at the time of such conduct as a result of mental disease or defect

Page 706

he [or she] lacks substantial capacity either to appreciate the criminality [wrongfulness] of his conduct or to conform his conduct to the requirements of law" (citation omitted).

The Model Jury Instructions on Homicide do not define the term "mental disease or defect." See Dunphe, 485 Mass. at 878-879. The instructions do clarify, however, that the phrase is a legal term that "need not fit into a formal medical diagnosis" (citation omitted). Id.

Kelly initially described a mental disease or defect as "words in the statute that determine criminal responsibility, so-called insanity in the state. And these terms were terms that were written in the early '60's, in which period of time mental diseases meant serious psychiatric conditions such as schizophrenia and manic depressive disorder, now bi-polar disorder." The defendant argues that, absent a curative instruction or further clarification from defense counsel, the jury would not have understood that they were not required to adopt any particular definition, or that experts differ in their definitions.

When Kelly mentioned "the statute" in describing a mental disease or defect, defense counsel objected on the ground that it was legal analysis. The prosecutor then asked Kelly to testify as to what the term "mental disease or defect" meant as a psychiatrist. Kelly explained that the term had been used in the early Twentieth Century and meant "serious mental conditions such as the model being diseases . . . includ[ing] conditions such as . . . schizophrenia, such as manic depressive disorder . . . . And those would be serious conditions that tend to have a biological component." Kelly then stated that, in his opinion, the defendant did not suffer from a mental disease or defect. Defense counsel did not object to this second definition.

Defense counsel later asked the judge to clarify for the jury the legal definition of "mental disease or defect." After the judge read aloud the model jury instruction on mental disease or defect, defense counsel apparently decided that the model instruction would sufficiently clarify the definition, and that his best course would be to comment on the definition in his closing. Thus, in his final charge, the judge instructed, "The phrase 'mental disease or defect' is a legal term, not a medical term. It need not fit into a formal medical diagnosis. . . . It is for you to determine in light of all the evidence whether the Defendant had a mental disease or defect."

Page 707

If a defense expert has testified concerning the McHoul test, see McHoul, 352 Mass. at 546-547, a Commonwealth expert may testify in rebuttal even if, in that expert's opinion, the defendant was not suffering from a mental disease or defect at the time of the commission of the offense. See Commonwealth v. Laliberty, 373 Mass. 238, 242 n.2 (1977). An expert's definition of "mental disease or defect" may be helpful to the jury, but the jury are not required to adopt any particular definition. Id. at 242. "The sole restriction placed on the admission of an expert's opinion concerning a defendant's mental state is that he [or she] may express an opinion only in accordance with the standard of the McHoul case." Id. at 243. While an expert may frame his or her testimony in terms of the McHoul test, it is preferable that the testimony be given in purely medical or psychological terms. See Commonwealth v. Shelley, 381 Mass. 340, 348 n.4 (1980), S.C., 411 Mass. 692 (1992).

Examining his testimony as a whole, Kelly permissibly defined the term "mental disease or defect." See Laliberty, 373 Mass. at 242. Kelly's testimony fit within Laliberty's sole restriction, as his description and his opinion addressed the defendant's mental state in accordance with the McHoul standard. See id. at 243. Although Kelly should not have mentioned the legal definition ("the statute"), the statement was brief, and he then reframed the definition in accordance with that used by a psychiatrist. To the extent that defense counsel was concerned that the jury would adopt the Commonwealth's definition, counsel could have asked any of the defendant's three expert witnesses to define the term. Moreover, the judge instructed the jury that the phrase "mental disease or defect" is a legal term that differs from the medical meaning of those words.

In sum, the expert's brief testimony concerning the legal definition of a mental disease or defect did not rise to the level of a substantial likelihood of a miscarriage of justice.

b. Instruction distinguishing between lack of criminal responsibility and diminished capacity. The defendant argues that the judge abused his discretion by not providing the jury a supplemental instruction distinguishing between a lack of criminal responsibility and diminished capacity. The defendant maintains that the failure to distinguish these concepts might have confused the jury and could have caused them to disregard evidence of diminished capacity if they first found that the defendant's mental condition did not rise to the level of a mental disease or defect.

Page 708

Because defense counsel requested such a supplemental instruction, we review for prejudicial error. See Commonwealth v. Biancardi, 421 Mass. 251, 253-254 (1995).

Judges have broad discretion in framing jury instructions, including determining the appropriate degree of elaboration. See Commonwealth v. Kelly, 470 Mass. 682, 688 (2015). Here, the judge asked defense counsel whether he believed that the 2013 Model Jury Instructions on Homicide adequately distinguished between a lack of criminal responsibility and diminished capacity. In response, counsel requested that the judge instruct the jury more clearly how they could distinguish between these concepts. The judge ultimately did not provide the requested supplemental instruction.

In his final charge, the judge instructed, based on the then newly adopted 2013 Model Jury Instructions on Homicide, that it was the Commonwealth's burden to prove

"One, that at the time of the alleged crime, the Defendant did not suffer from a mental disease or defect, or;

"Two, that if the Defendant did suffer from a mental disease or defect, he nonetheless retained the substantial capacity to appreciate the wrongfulness or criminality of his conduct and to conform his conduct to the requirements of the law, or;

"Three, that if the Defendant lacked the substantial capacity to appreciate the wrongfulness or criminality of his conduct, and to conform his conduct to the requirements of the law, his lack of such capacity was solely the result of voluntary intoxication by alcohol or other drugs, or;

"Four, that if the Defendant lacked the substantial capacity I have just described due to a combination of mental disease or defect and his voluntary consumption of alcohol or other drugs, then he knew or should have known that his use of the substances would interact with his mental disease or defect and cause him to lose such capacity.

"If one of those four circumstances have been proved beyond a reasonable doubt, then the government has satisfied its burden beyond a reasonable doubt to establish the Defendant's legal sanity."

The judge then went on to explain that a mental disease or defect is a legal term, and that the Commonwealth was required to prove

that the defendant had not been suffering from a mental disease or defect at the time of the stabbing.

The judge later instructed on mental impairment as follows:

"In deciding whether the Defendant intended to kill the victim . . . and whether he formed that intent with deliberate premeditation, you may consider any credible evidence that the Defendant suffered a mental impairment or was affected by his consumption of alcohol or drugs. A Defendant may form the required intent and act with deliberate premeditation even if he suffered from a mental impairment . . . ."

The judge also explained that the jury could consider evidence of the defendant's mental impairment in determining whether he had acted with deliberate premeditation or extreme atrocity or cruelty.

While perhaps less than pellucid, the judge's instructions adequately distinguished between the concepts of mental disease or defect and mental impairment. Considering the instructions as a whole, these two concepts were presented to the jury as two different factors they should consider. The jury were told that, to prove the defendant was criminally responsible, the Commonwealth bore the burden of proving, beyond a reasonable doubt, that the defendant did not have a mental disease or defect. They later were instructed that the defendant's mental impairment could have affected his ability to form the required intent.

It is possible that the jury confused these two concepts, as the distinction between them is elusive. See Commonwealth v. Bishop, 461 Mass. 586, 600 (2012). To the extent that the jury did confuse these issues, any such confusion was unlikely to rise to the level of prejudicial error. The Commonwealth's case was very strong, and throughout the trial, the jury heard extensive evidence concerning the defendant's premeditated intent. On the day before the stabbing, for instance, the defendant tried to fly to Nantucket with a large kitchen knife, and proffered four different explanations, none of them reasonable, when airport security asked why he had had the knife. [Note 4] The jury also heard that, on the day of the stabbing, immediately after arriving on Nantucket, the defendant drove to a surf shop and purchased several knives; he

Page 710

had obtained directions to that shop from another store, which did not sell knives. Moreover, the jury heard that, before going to the cottage, the defendant approached the victim's landlord and inquired whether the victim was at home, and then headed toward the cottage notwithstanding the landlord's equivocal response. In addition, the nature of the twenty-three stab wounds covering the victim's torso, nose, arms, and hands, and the deoxyribonucleic acid match between the victim and the blood found on one of the knives the defendant had purchased, would have allowed the jury to infer an intent to kill, as they were instructed they could do, from the use of a dangerous weapon in this manner.

In sum, while the judge chose not to provide an additional instruction distinguishing between mental impairment and mental disease or defect, the judge did define both of those terms in language consistent with the Model Jury Instructions on Homicide. There was no error.

c. *Inferring malice from the use of a dangerous weapon.* The defendant argues that the judge should not have instructed the jury that they could infer malice from the intentional use of a dangerous weapon. Specifically, the defendant contends that the instruction impermissibly elevated the element of malice above other elements of murder in the first degree, and that it relieved the Commonwealth of its burden to prove malice. The defendant also maintains that the instruction subverted testimony by his expert that, at the time of the stabbing, the defendant was incapable of understanding the consequences of his actions. Because the defendant objected to the provision of this instruction, we review for prejudicial error. See Odgren, 483 Mass. at 46.

Under our existing jurisprudence, a jury may infer an intent to kill from the use of a dangerous weapon against another, even where there is evidence of a defendant's intoxication or mental impairment. See id. See also Commonwealth v. Miller, 457 Mass. 69, 74-75 (2010). The instruction on such an inference must tell the jury that they may infer malice, and may not instruct the jury that they must draw such an inference. Odgren, supra at 47.

Here, the judge instructed the jury on the elements of murder in the first degree, on theories of premeditation and extreme atrocity or cruelty. The judge then instructed on the three prongs of malice and the elements of murder in the second degree. Before instructing on the inference that they could draw from the use of a dangerous weapon, the judge explained:

"If the Commonwealth has proved beyond a reasonable doubt the two elements necessary for second degree murder and has proved beyond a reasonable doubt the Defendant's legal sanity, then you may convict. If the Commonwealth has failed to prove any of those matters beyond a reasonable doubt, then you may not convict of second degree murder."

The judge then gave the disputed instruction regarding the inference that the jury could draw from the intentional use of a dangerous weapon against another, in language that hewed closely to the wording that then had been newly modified in the 2013 Model Jury Instructions on Homicide:

"As a general rule, ladies and gentlemen, you are permitted, but are not required[,] to infer that a person who intentionally uses a dangerous weapon on another person intends to kill that person or cause him grievous bodily harm or intends to do an act which in the circumstances known to him a reasonable person would know creates a plain and strong likelihood that death would result."

The judge also later instructed the jury that they could consider manslaughter if the Commonwealth failed to prove murder in the first degree and murder in the second degree. He described the elements of voluntary manslaughter and explained that the Commonwealth had to prove each of those elements, and the defendant's legal sanity, beyond a reasonable doubt.

There was no error in the instruction that the jury could, but need not, infer an intent to kill from the intentional use of a dangerous weapon in the circumstances here. The instruction essentially quoted the then-applicable Model Jury Instructions on Homicide concerning the use of a dangerous weapon. See Model Jury Instructions on Homicide 92 (2013). We previously have noted with approval the inference that may be drawn from the use of a dangerous weapon, even where there is evidence of a defendant's intoxication or mental impairment. See, e.g., Odgren, 483 Mass. 47-49; Miller, 457 Mass. at 74; Commonwealth v. Oliveira, 445 Mass. 837, 842-845 (2006).

Beginning in 2013, the introduction to the supplemental instruction on the inference the jury might draw from the use of a dangerous weapon against the person of another added a requirement that, before instructing on such an inference, the judge had to determine from the evidence at trial that "the nature of the dangerous weapon used and the manner of its use reasonably

supports" the inference. The 2013 Model Jury Instructions on Homicide also noted that, before giving the instruction, the judge should consider "the type of dangerous weapon and the manner in which it was used in the circumstances of the case, and should only give this instruction where the nature of the weapon and the manner of its use reasonably supports the inference." See Commonwealth v. Colas, 486 Mass. 831, 842-843 (2021), citing Commonwealth v. Tu Trinh, 458 Mass. 776, 784 nn.12, 13 (2011) ("As a general rule, the jury are permitted to infer an intent to kill from the use of a dangerous weapon. . . . The reasonableness of this inference depends, as set forth in the model jury instructions on homicide, upon 'the nature of the dangerous weapon and the manner of its use'" [citation omitted]).

While the judge did not make an explicit finding to this effect, the nature of the twenty-three penetrating stab wounds all over the victim's torso, nose, hands, and arms, the blood on walls, floors, and surfaces throughout the cottage, and the newly purchased knife that was discarded in the bushes near where the defendant left his rental vehicle fully support a determination that the circumstances warranted giving this instruction. At a sidebar discussion concerning the judge's final charge, the attorneys and the judge discussed at some length the changes in this instruction, favorable to defendants, to remove the use of the word "malice," which had appeared in the prior version of the instructions.

As the defendant points out, courts in some jurisdictions have discontinued the use of such an inference. See, e.g., State v. Burdette, 427 S.C. 490, 504-505 (2019) ("Regardless of the evidence presented at trial, trial courts shall not instruct a jury that the element of malice may be inferred when the deed is done with a deadly weapon"). In reaching this decision, the South Carolina Supreme Court explained, "When the trial court tells the jury it may use evidence of the use of a deadly weapon to establish the existence of malice, a critical element of the charge of murder, the trial court has directly commented upon facts in evidence, elevated those facts, and emphasized them to the jury." Id. at 502. The Appeals Court similarly has held that "the court in all cases should be scrupulously careful not to invade the province of the jury by undertaking to decide on the weight or effect of evidence." Commonwealth v. Cote, 5 Mass. App. Ct. 365, 369-370 (1977) (judge "shall not charge juries with respect to matters of fact" or "direct what inferences the jury should draw from certain evidence" [citation omitted]).

Page 713

Of course, the instruction on the inference that may be drawn does not direct the jury to make such an inference. And here, the evidence of malice was overwhelming, and there was no need to draw an inference from the use of a knife that the defendant intended to kill the victim. The twenty-three wounds to the victim's torso, nose, arms, and hands, leaving blood on walls, floors, and fixtures throughout the cottage, in conjunction with the defendant's efforts to obtain the knife on arrival, to delay discovery of the victim's body by closing up the cottage, to dispose of the weapon after the attack, and to flee the scene all supported a finding of an intent to kill.

The defendant also argues that certain instructions differed impermissibly from the instructions given in Miller. In Miller, 457 Mass. at 70, 72, the defendant was being tried on a charge of murder in the first degree and pursued a defense of intoxication and mental impairment. Because the victim had been killed with a hammer, the judge also instructed on the inference the jury could draw from the use of a dangerous weapon. Id. at 71-74. Following that instruction, the judge told the jury, "I reiterate, whenever the Commonwealth must prove that the defendant intended to do something . . . , you may consider any credible evidence of mental impairment . . . in determining . . . the defendant's intent or knowledge beyond a reasonable doubt."

The defendant contends that the judge should have provided a similar instruction in this case, which would have directed the jury to consider mental impairment and intoxication whenever the Commonwealth was required to prove intent. We do not agree. Prior to instructing on the elements of murder, the judge gave an instruction, following the 2013 Model Jury Instructions on Homicide, that the jury "may consider any credible evidence that the Defendant suffered a mental impairment or was affected by his consumption of alcohol or drugs." We previously have affirmed the use of such an instruction. See Oliveira, 445 Mass. 845-846. Moreover, immediately prior to, and immediately following, the instruction on the possible inference to be drawn from the use of a dangerous weapon, the judge instructed the jury that the Commonwealth was required to prove the defendant's mental state beyond a reasonable doubt.

Accordingly, there was no error in the instruction on the inference of an intent to kill that the jury could draw from the use of a dangerous weapon.

d. *Instruction that defendant was incapable of resisting urge to consume drugs and alcohol.* The defendant also contends that the jury should have been instructed to consider whether he was incapable of resisting the urge to consume drugs or alcohol, regardless of whether he was aware of negative interactions between his consumption of drugs or alcohol and his mental state. The defendant maintains that such an instruction should have been given when the jury were instructed that he was criminally responsible if he knew that substances such as drugs and alcohol would interact with his mental disease or defect and would cause him to lose the capacity to conform his conduct to the law. See DiPadova, 460 Mass. at 439-440

(Appendix) (establishing so-called DiPadova instruction). In the alternative, the defendant argues that the DiPadova instruction should have been omitted entirely. We do not agree.

As the defendant did not request a DiPadova instruction, and did not object to the instruction given, we review to determine whether the absence of the requested instruction created a substantial likelihood of a miscarriage of justice. See Commonwealth v. The Ngoc Tran, 471 Mass. 179, 183-184 (2015).

For almost fifty years, we have held that drug addiction, by itself, does not qualify as a mental disease or defect that could support a finding of a lack of criminal responsibility. See Commonwealth v. Sheehan, 376 Mass. 765, 767-769 (1978). A drug-induced or exacerbated mental disease or defect, however, ultimately may result from the use of a prescription drug, an illegal drug, the chronic abuse of alcohol, a physical illness, or a genetic disorder. See Dunphe, 485 Mass. at 880-881. The origins of the disease or defect are irrelevant. See id. Moreover, where a defendant has a mental disease or defect such that the defendant lacks the capacity to conform his or her conduct to the law, the consumption of alcohol or drugs does not preclude the defense of a lack of criminal responsibility. See Commonwealth v. Muller, 477 Mass. 415, 428 (2017).

A lack of criminal capacity, arising from the long-term abuse of alcohol, has been recognized as establishing a lack of criminal responsibility. See Dunphe, 485 Mass. at 880-881, and cases cited. In addition, where a defendant has a mental disease or defect that, by itself, does not render the defendant incapable of understanding the wrongfulness of his or her conduct, and conforming that conduct to the law, the consumption of drugs or alcohol in conjunction with the mental disease or defect may result in the defendant being unable to do so. When the consumption of drugs or alcohol exacerbates a mental condition such that the

Page 715

interaction of the drugs or alcohol with the condition causes a defendant to lack the substantial capacity, and the defendant does not know, or have reason to know, that the consumption of drugs or alcohol would trigger the exacerbation in his or her mental condition, the defendant is not criminally responsible. See id. at 882. By contrast, if the Commonwealth were able to prove, beyond a reasonable doubt, that a defendant knew or had reason to know that the consumption of alcohol or drugs would so exacerbate his or her mental condition, then the defendant would be criminally responsible. See id.

In response to the defendant's request, the judge here gave the DiPadova instruction, including the following:

"A Defendant who lost the substantial capacity I have just described after he consumed drugs or alcohol and who knew or had reason to know that his consumption would trigger or intensify in him a mental disease or defect that could cause him to lack that capacity is criminally responsible for his resulting conduct."

This instruction properly informed the jury of their ability to determine the defendant's degree of criminal responsibility by considering his mental disease or defect and its interaction with his consumption of drugs and alcohol. The defendant points to no case, in the Commonwealth or in any other jurisdiction, where the requested instruction -- that the jury consider whether the defendant was incapable of resisting the urge to use substances -- has been given, and we are aware of none. Rather, the defendant's requested instruction in some respects contravenes this court's holding in Sheehan, 376 Mass. at 767-769, that drug addiction, standing alone, and being "blacked out" from drug addiction does not establish a mental disease or defect that would warrant a finding of not guilty by reason of insanity.

In support of his argument that the additional instruction should have been given, the defendant points out that the science relied upon in Sheehan is outdated and no longer reflects current scientific understanding. In Sheehan, 376 Mass. at 766-767, the defendant argued that drug addiction was a mental disease that, without more, would warrant a finding of not guilty by reason of a lack of criminal responsibility. Rejecting this argument, the court explained:

"The essential consideration is not whether the medical profession characterizes drug addiction as a mental disease or defect but rather whether our society should relieve from criminal responsibility a drug addict who at the time of the commission of the crime was unable to conform his conduct to the requirements of law because of his addiction."

Id. at 769. The court noted that, in some circumstances, an individual with a substance use disorder may be relieved of responsibility for criminal conduct, such as when the user's lack of criminal capacity is not a result of the addiction. Id. But the court rejected the view that addiction alone is sufficient to support a finding that the consumption of the drugs was involuntary. Id. at 771. In support, the court pointed to research by Herbert Fingarette. See Fingarette, Addiction and Criminal Responsibility, 84 Yale L.J. 413, 443 (1975). Fingarette's findings regarding addiction subsequently have been widely denounced. See, e.g., Roberts, Herbert Fingarette, Contrarian Philosopher on Alcoholism, Dies at 97, N.Y. Times, Nov. 15, 2018.

As the defendant emphasizes, a number of decisions by this court and the Appeals Court since Sheehan was issued have recognized addiction as a disease that "may affect an individual's urge to use substances." Commonwealth v. Eldred, 480 Mass. 90, 94 n.6 (2018). See, e.g., Dunphe, 485 Mass. at 880-883, and cases cited; Commonwealth v. Peno, 485 Mass. 378, 388 (2020); Commonwealth v. Plasse, 481 Mass. 199, 205-208 (2019), and cases cited. The defendant's argument that there was a substantial likelihood of a miscarriage of justice because the requested instruction was not given, however, is unavailing.

Regardless of whether the science relied upon in Sheehan is outdated, there was ample evidence before the jury to support a finding that the defendant's conduct was knowing and intentional, and undertaken after substantial planning, notwithstanding his evident intoxication at the time of the attack. On this record, the jury could have found that the defendant's level of intoxication, in conjunction with his mental health issues, did not negate his ability to plan and carry out a premeditated attack on the victim, attempt to conceal the evidence of the attack, and then drive a vehicle on a State highway with no apparent impairment in his ability to comply with the traffic laws. The judge did not err in instructing the jury consistently with DiPadova, and certainly did not create a substantial likelihood of a miscarriage of justice in relying upon instructions we recently affirmed.

e. Review under G. L. c. 278, § 33E. The defendant also asks that we exercise our authority under G. L. c. 278, § 33E, to grant him extraordinary relief. Having carefully reviewed the record, we discern no reason to order a new trial or to reduce the degree of guilt.

Judgments affirmed.

FOOTNOTES

[Note 1] Police later found the knife and the victim's wallet in a bush next to the vehicle, and bottles of beer inside the vehicle.

[Note 2] One of the defendant's experts testified at trial concerning the medications the defendant had been prescribed, their side effects, and their potential interactions. Klonopin is a brand of clonazepam. It can be used to treat seizures, panic disorders, anxiety, and mania. It may cause paranoia and impair memory, judgment, and coordination. Clonazepam is a benzodiazepine and should not be mixed with alcohol. Doing so may slow or suppress breathing, possibly resulting in death. See United States Food and Drug Administration, Klonopin Tablets (clonazepam), https://www.accessdata.fda.gov/drugsatfda_docs/label/2021/017533s061lbl.pdf [https://perma.cc/CSV9-CZXM]; National Library of Medicine, Clonazepam, https://www.ncbi.nlm.nih.gov/books/NBK556010 [https://perma.cc/T7HK-L73S].

[Note 3] Zoloft is a selective serotonin reuptake inhibitor that can be used to treat depression, obsessive-compulsive disorder, posttraumatic stress disorder, and panic disorder. It should not be mixed with alcohol. See United States Food and Drug Administration, Sertraline (marketed as Zoloft) Information, https://www.fda.gov/drugs/postmarket-drug-safety-information-patients-and-providers/sertraline-marketed-zoloft-information [https://perma.cc/P3TR-DWAT]; National Library of Medicine, Sertraline, https://www.ncbi.nlm.nih.gov/books/NBK547689 [https://perma.cc/CY2Z-DBGL]. There was no testimony at trial as to the dosage of the Klonopin pills in the bottle found in the defendant's rental vehicle or how much he was supposed to take each day. There was testimony as to the amount of Zoloft he was to take per day; in June of 2004, that dosage had been increased from fifty to one hundred milligrams.

[Note 4] The defendant variously said that he brought the knife to cut a cake, that he was taking it to go fishing or to cut fish, that he forgot he had the knife with him, and that his sister had asked him to bring a knife to cut a turkey.

Absent an appeal to the U.S. Supreme Court, or a gubernatorial pardon, Mr. Toolan would appear to have exhausted all the justice that money can buy. But the public had long ago written off any chance for a successful appeal of the second conviction. The following mock epitaph appeared online after the first trial, its author(s) evidently preferring to remain anonymous:

My name was Tommy Toolan.
I said I wasn't foolin'.
The woman didn't buy it.
She thought I'd never try it.

I felt that I was scot-free.
It seemed they hadn't caught me.
I'd thrown away the knife, see.
Forgot my pants were bloody.

So then in jail I'm mewlin'.
The grind was really gruelin'.
'Twas Rue Morgue, not Rue Moulin.
My life's thread was unspoolin'.

Goodbye, Mr. Goodbar.

www.ingramcontent.com/pod-product-compliance
Lightning Source LLC
Chambersburg PA
CBHW022132170526
45157CB00004B/1849